GEMST
and
OCCULT POWERS

James Sturzaker

METATRON PUBLICATIONS

First Published 1977
Second Impression 1980

ISBN 0 9506168 0 X

Cover screen printed by hand
Printed by Nirvana Press, England

GEMSTONES

From ancient times Gemstones have played an important part in healing, but even more so in Ritual. They have been used by the orthodox and unorthodox in all aspects of worship both with invocation and evocation.

This book sets out planetary and zodiac relationships and also the corresponden-ces with some of the Archangels which are of importance in Occult Ritual.

Birthstones are listed by month and by zodiacal sign making it simple to choose a personal gemstone and the gemstones for each day are also to be found.

For those interested in natural healing methods, details of how to prepare the stones together with their therapeutic uses are clearly stated.

Full list of publications sent on request

METATRON PUBLICATIONS,

25 CIRCLE GARDENS,

MERTON PARK,

LONDON SW19 3JX.

By the same author:

KABBALISTIC APHORISMS

COLOUR AND THE KABBALAH
(with Doreen Sturzaker)

THE TWELVE RAYS

FIRST STEPS TO KABBALAH

AROMATICS IN RITUAL AND
THERAPEUTICS

CONTENTS

DIAGRAMS

Many articles and books have been written on this subject all down the ages, just as Man has revered them as far back as history can be traced.

Reference to these fascinating and beautiful intelligencies of the Mineral Kingdom can be found in the fields of religion, philosophy, therapeutics and magic. What is their attraction? Very few human beings can resist gemstones. What is their magic and mystery that no true occultist can overlook them?

Part of their power lies in their physical composition, the various chemical compounds that make up their structure being integrated with the great Cosmic Rays from which they obtain their colour.

The Rays in themselves are a lifetimes study and yet they only form one aspect of the Royal Family of the Mineral Kingdom. To even scratch the surface of the occult nature of gemstones a knowledge of the Rays and their qualities is essential.

It has been said, that before the fall of Man, the Earths aura was fluidic and, at the time of his fall into dense matter, this aura also densified and shattered into many pieces which we know of today as gemstones.

A pretty and fascinating thought, but it must be assumed to be far from the

3

truth; **Man even before the fall did not possess the mystical power of the gems.**

Part of their attraction lies in the living colour that emanates from them; even the lowliest, if one can say any single gem is lowlier than the others, gives forth a living sparkle of cosmic energy that is locked up inside the heart of it.

Purely from a material value, a lowly gem like the heamatite when polished has a sparkle that makes even its black colour a living cosmic force vibrant with life.

Locked within their crystaline outer covering is the secret of the wisdom of all the ages, hence their association with the Tree of Life and with the "Revelations".

If we could unlock and obtain all the secrets held within each gemstone we would be walking with the Gods, but we only understand them at the level of consciousness that we as individuals have reached.

The term gemstones is used in both the heading and the text because all stones have their occult properties for good and evil and it is not my intention to limit this article to the precious stones.

One thing that must be quite clear, no gemstone is evil in itself; ill luck or ill health only befalls the wearer of any stone when that individual's vibrations are out of harmony with those of the gem being worn or possessed.

A great deal has been written about the misfortunes that come to people who wear or posess an opal. This is a much maligned gem and unfairly called an unlucky stone. It is, on the contrary, one of the most helpful gems if the owner is in harmony with its vibrations.

What is so unfortunate is that very few human beings are in vibratory harmony with the opal, but this is the fault of Man, not the gem. The state of inharmonius relations between Man and the opal is directly connected with "The Rays".

Where the opal combines a balance of all the rays and so has a perfect balance of the cosmic forces, Man has invariably one Ray which is predominant and so his vibrations are not so delicately balanced as those of the opal.

Just as Man is bound up inextricably with colour and astrology so are the gemstones. Gemstones are related to astrology by their colour content and follow the same principle as colour and aromatics; the dark gems are at the bass end of the scale and the lighter shades on the higher or treble end of the scale.

One of the finest books to study for research into the value of gemstone vibrations is the Bible. It must, however, be studied at the esoteric level.

If this is done much valuable knowledge will be gained. If read purely on the physical level no satisfactory knowledge will accrue and the student will be left with a quantity of signs and symbols without any apparent meaning.

It might be helpful at this point to give a few interesting incidents in relation to the power of gems and effects on individuals.

President Kruger possessed a diamond that had been the property of Chaka, a Zulu Chief. Chaka was assassinated by his brother in order to possess the diamond. Kruger was the sixteenth person to possess this particular gem and each previous owner had died a violent death. Kruger's own misfortunes were credited to the possession of this stone. Misfortunes befalling one owner, even two or three owners, may be coincidence. Can coincidence stretch to sixteen owners?

The breast-plate of the High Priest created and held great influence over the Jews and a tradition developed that on the Day of Atonement the High Priest asked forgiveness for the sins of his people; if forgiven the stones of the Urim and Thummim sparkled with brightness; if, however, forgiveness was not forthcoming the precious stones lost what sparkle they had and became very dark in colour. Because of this occult phenomena the Magi of the East maintained that there were magical and virtuous

6

properties contained within the stones of the breast-plate.

Plato around 400 B.C. accepted the precious stones as containing the vivifying spirits who normally dwelt in the stars. It may be from this origin that certain occult groups believe in the fall of the gemstones even today.

There was at one time, and may still be today, a stone preserved in the Abbey at St. Albans. It was presented by the Bishop of Ardfert, Ireland. This precious stone is called the Serpent's Stone; it is of a light airy colour and marked with white spots.

There was at one time in the Church of Old St. Pauls, London, a sapphire. This was used for helping all those with eye troubles who cared to use it.

From earliest times there has been an affinity between the gemstones and religion. This still exists today, particularly in the Roman Catholic Church. The Pope always has an amethyst ring (in colour this is a very devotional ray). The Cardinals are presented with a sapphire ring on their elevation. The sapphire was the stone chosen or used for the tablets which Moses received containing the Ten Commandments.

Dr. Butler, a well known Irish physician of last century, is reputed to have possessed a small stone (type not specified) with which marvellous cures were brought about. The stone was plunged into almond oil; the oil absorbed its curative vibrations and was so potent that a spoonful of the liquid in many cases was sufficient to cure the illness. Testament to its efficacy was given by a Franciscan friar who received a cure from Erysipelas.

Many more instances could be quoted of unusual happenings associated with the gem stones. All through the ages they have been revered for reasons other than financial. The most appropriate summing up of their unknown power is that made by Bacon: "Many things that operate upon the spirits of man by secret sympathy and antipathy. That the Precious Stones have virtues in the wearing has been anciently and generally received; so much is true that gems have fine spirits as appears by their splendour; and therefore they may operate on the spirits of men to strengthen and exhilarate them". "It is manifest, moreover, that light, above all things, rejoices the spirits of men, and varied light has the same effect, which may be one cause why Precious Stones exhilarate".

It is of interest to note Bacon's remarks about light and colour in light; in his mind the association of colour to the gemstones was an integral part of their power. This applies also in the mineral content, which emits from the gems its own vibrations. Man is, therefore, receiving from the Gemstones the vibrations of both colour and minerals plus the vibrations applicable to the stone itself. With this combination the gems are possessed of a power that can be used, but is inexplicable and can only be referred to as their occult power.

From whatever source the power of the gems is derived, and whatever their origin may have been, they still possess and exercise an influence on mankind.

The twelve precious stones corresponding to those in the breast-plate of the High Priest have an aspect that is similar to the planets. There are seven sacred and five non-sacred gems.

The seven transparent and translucent are the sacred; the five opaque are the non-sacred. It will be noted that there are seven and five also in the foundations of the Holy City.

The Diamond is the synthesizing stone containing all virtues and properties of the other twelve. The following table sets out the twelve gems and their positions in the Breast Plate of the High Priest and the foundations of the New Jerusalem.

Gemstone	Position in the High Priest's Breast Plate	Foundations of the Holy City
Bloodstone	12	1
Sapphire	5	2
Agate	8	3
Emerald	3	4
Onyx	6	5
Cornelian	1	6
Chrysolite	10	7
Beryl	11	8
Topaz	2	9
Turquoise	4	10
Garnet	7	11
Amethyst	9	12

As the signs of the Zodiac are indicative of twelve types of the human race with modifications, so the twelve foundations are symbolic of the twelve virtues that must be acquired for each individual to reach a stage of vibratory harmony.

The gemstones contain the characteristics and qualities of both and therefore their vibrations in the therapeutical field are of immense value as they can work at the physical level, the mental level and even at the higher spiritual level.

It is appropriate at this stage to give a few of the qualities and characteristics for each of the twelve.

First Foundation - Aries - Bloodstone

The Bloodstone is assigned to St. Peter - "On this rock I build my Church", the rock being the first foundation. The qualities of Peter were courage and determination, typical of the Aries type. The Bloodstone is useful for strengthening the will and bestowing courage; this is using the therapeutical value on the mental level. Courage and will are certainly two of the first qualities to be acquired when building the physical temple and when stepping out on the occult and spiritual path.

Second Foundation - Taurus - Sapphire

The Sapphire formed the second foundation of the Holy City. One of the attributes contained within the vibrations of the Sapphire is faith. This stone is also representative of the Apostle Andrew who was also noted for his Heavenly faith. These facts tend to confirm that to make the physical body a holy temple faith must be cultivated after the first foundation of rock has been established. On the higher level of therapeutics the Sapphire would be indicated for all cases where lack of faith is a contributory factor of the illness.

Third Foundation - Gemini - Agate

The twins of Gemini signify two pillars of wisdom - the higher and lower mind. James the son of Zebedee and brother of John was possessed of wisdom and it seems fitting that the Agate which bestows the vibrations of wisdom should be the gemstone of both the Apostle and the sign and also the attribute of the third foundation. In the therapeutical field the Agate would be used where the physical disharmony is caused through unwise living. It would be futile to cure the disease without helping the patient to obtain wisdom in living.

Fourth Foundation - Cancer - Emerald

The characteristics of the Emerald are fearlessness and gentleness. It is also emblematical of truth. Virtues of the Apostle John and those bestowed by the zodiacal sign of Cancer bear a great similarity to those of the Emerald. The main virtue is, of course, gentleness and sympathy and what better virtues for the fourth foundation of our physical temple. The therapeutical value of this gemstone is rather obvious. On the higher levels it should be used for all cases where selfishness, lack of consideration and like characteristics are the basis of illness.

Fifth Foundation - Leo - Onyx

Phillip was the friendly Apostle, full of love and faith. This is typical of the Leo sign and corresponds to the virtue of the Onyx whose vibrations are such as to drive out temper and all that is hateful. Friendship to all living creatures forms this fifth foundation and the therapeutical value of the Onyx lies in its ability to create friendly feelings by casting out temper and hate.

Sixth Foundation - Virgo - Cornelian

Makes cheerful minds, expels fears, gives courage, prevents strife and anger. That is the Cornelian in a nutshell, giving all the time, the epitome of self sacrifice; so it is with the sign Virgo, the path of virtue. Bartholomew was the Apostle of self sacrifice; although not perhaps so well known as some of his fellow apostles, his was the path of virtue and so from ancient times his name has been connected to Virgo and the Cornelian. On the higher therapeutical levels this stone should be used for patients whose root cause of illness is greed; self-centred individuals whose life is built on possessions - the "I have", "I want" types.

Libra is the sign of balance, poise, harmony, beauty in all things, the wisdom that gives purity of balance. The Apostle Matthias had a purity of character that attracted the chrysolite as emplematic of his vibrations, this gem stone being noted for the emission of vibrations that induce purity. Therapeutic use of this stone is for all patients with a "guilt" complex at the root of their disease.

Eighth foundation - Scorpio - Beryl

The Beryl increases conjugal love. It also strengthens convictions. It was for the latter attribute that the ancients assigned this gem stone to the Apostle Thomas who was so lacking in this quality. Perhaps for the same reason the ancients named Thomas as representative of the zodiacal sign Scorpio. Numbered amongst the qualities of this sign are those of strong conviction and intense, profound fidelity.

In the therapeutical field the Beryl can be used to advantage where the patient lacks conviction in himself, but most of all lacks conviction in his ability to be physically fit, the patient who comes for help but feels his case is hopeless.

James the less was the Apostle noted for his delicacy, and for this reason he was associated with the Topaz and the sign Sagittarius. James possessed the inner radiance of the Topaz and the aspiration that gives freedom of the soul that belongs to Sagittarius. From these qualities is derived that delicacy that is little short of perfection. All patients where the root cause of illness lies in their grossness, uncouthness of speech and a mind that is full of filth should be given treatment that includes the benificial Topaz.

Tenth Foundation - Capricorn - Turquoise

Capricorn emits the vibrations of sweetness, the sweet temper that is developed by taking a wide view, always prepared to help those on the lower levels to reach the peaks. The vibrations of the Turquoise are possessed of the same qualities with an accent on sympathy for the sick. The Apostle Simon was the sum total of these attributes and became known for his sweet temper. Where illness is caused by bad temper, resentment and other similar mental toxins Turquoise should be used.

Eleventh Foundation - Aquarius - Garnet

From the Garnet and the Zodiacal sign Aquarius emanate the vibrations that create serenity through the repression of vanity and excess luxury, creates the interest in the whole of humanity and a concern for humanity and its welfare. The Apostle Thaddeus acquired this quality of serenity. To use the Garnet in the field of natural therapeutics for nervous cases is ideal and it should bring great relief to the sufferer.

Twelfth Foundation - Pisces - Amethyst

Sobriety is the keynote of Matthew, the sobriety that develops the quality of greatness, gentleness, compassion, universal love, peace, tranquility and compassionate insight, all the qualities that link Matthews' name with the sign Pisces and the gemstone Amethyst.

In this last foundation are embodied many of the qualities of the earlier foundations. This is one of the reasons why the Amethyst is such a spiritual gemstone. It is invaluable in the practice of Gemtherapy but in therapeutical use it should be handled with care because of its very high and potent vibrations. It should be used chiefly in those cases where illness or disharmony is caused by excess.

The twelve foundations or mental qualities having been explained, it may be appropriate at this point to give a diagram that shows the perfect city of health.

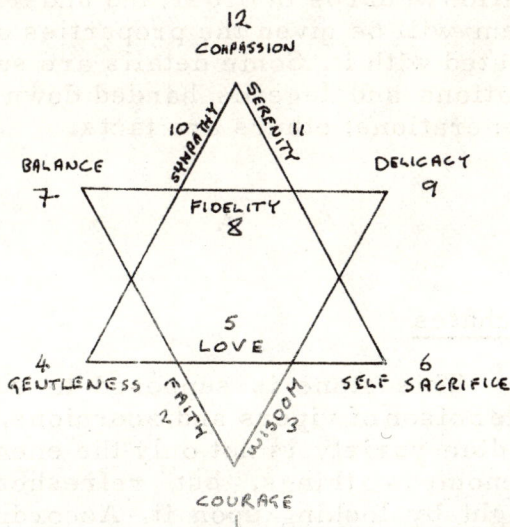

Vibrations of courage tempered by faith and wisdom give delicacy and balance combined with fidelity. Gentleness through Love gives the vibrations of self sacrifice. Gentleness extends to sympathy and self sacrifice to serenity and the sum total of all these vibrations is the synthesising quality of compassion.

Alphabetical Listing of Gemstones

Having taken a general survey of the gemstones a more detailed examination would be in order and under each gem will be given the properties associated with it. Some details are superstitions and legends handed down over generations; others are facts.

A

Achates

This stone is supposed to subdue the poison of vipers and scorpions. The Indian variety is not only the enemy of venomous things, but refreshes the sight by looking upon it. According to Leonardus, the physician to the Borgias, if held in the mouth it quenches thirst. It also turns away storms and puts a stop to lightning. This stone has an affinity with Myrrh if it is the Persian species; they are credited as both being on the same ray which is the White ray.

Agapis

This gem, if bound to the wound of scorpion stings or viper bites is supposed to bring about a cure; dipped in water and rubbed over the wound it immediately takes away or mitigates the pain.

Agate

Cooling, useful for fevers, quenches the thirst and steadies the pulse. If worn regularly it ensures good health and acts as a charm against spiders and scorpions. It is supposed to be good for athletes, is a bringer of good luck, wealth, longevity and happiness. Like the Alectoria it confers eloquence but on both man and woman, it enlightens the mind. In olden times it was believed that the fumes of an agate would avert a tempest, and even up to a hundred years ago, the old apothecaries used powdered agate mixed with water as an antidote for the venom of serpents. It is recorded as being one of the stones in the High Priest's Breastplate. The prophet Isaiah mentions it when he says, "I will make thy windows of Agate", in other words bringing light or enlightening the mind. It was used as a protection against thunder, sorcery, fiendish possessions, poison, intoxicants, skin diseases and nightmares. The ancients took the agate and used it as a symbol of the third eye. It can be used as a charm to protect its wearer from falling and it can also banish fear. It is the gem for the researcher; worn against the skin it makes him susceptible to new ideas. The Archangel Bariel has a close connection with this stone.

Alectoria

A crystalline coloured stone, a little darkish, somewhat resembling limpid water and sometimes has flesh coloured veins running through it. If held in the mouth allays thirst. Is credited with making its wearer invisible. The Alectoria makes a wife agreeable to her husband and renders a man eloquent, constant and agreeable.

Alexandrite

Very little is known about this particular gemstone and as it was only discovered in the early 19th Century very little superstition or legend has been attached to it. It is, however, regarded as a gem that gives deep devotion to the wearer and is also supposed to be a bringer of luck. Although it is of the transparent variety it emits two colours, by day an amethyst colouring, and at night it gives off a shade of emerald green.

Amber

This gem is not a mineral as the others but is a fossil resin. In spite of

this difference it is revered and has
attached to it many virtues. It is supposed to be good for the fires of the
soul and as a talisman will protect the
wearer from witchcraft and sorcery
and will drive away adders. The curative powers of amber cover a very
wide field. It can be found useful for
eye affections, good for lungs and kidneys, and has on occasions proved
useful to the liver. Oil of amber can
be of benefit in infantile convulsions and
is useful for coughs. Asthma, dropsy
and toothache are also supposed to respond to this gemstone. Amber will
attract things to itself except where oil
has been smeared upon them. Glandular
swellings of the throat can be alleviated
by amber, but if worn as a charm the
majority of diseases will never occur
as it is a charm against disease and
infection. On the top of all these virtues
it is lucky for the wearer and makes
them attractive to the opposite sex.
Although not the main gemstone of the
Sun it does have a correlation with it.

Amethyst

The amethyst is of the quartz
variety; a gem worn in the rings of
Bishops and it is often called "The
Bishops Ring". It is much used in the
temples of the East. The amethyst is
the principal stone of the 7th Ray which

21

is the mystical and ceremonial ray, perhaps this is the explanation as to the priesthoods attachment to it. Amongst its attributes is the virtue of bestowing mental peace. It is also synonymous with chastity and has the power to preserve its wearer from intoxicants. The ancients called the amethyst "the gem of Venus" or "the gem of fire". It is credited with the power to destroy evil thoughts. Amethyst drapes are useful to calm the mind of the insane and it is recorded that Beethoven gained inspiration from and composed his fine works in a room of amethyst drapes. One of the chief virtues of the amethyst is a deep love and it can help to cement broken friendships. Will power is strengthened by the amethyst; it gives courage and preserves from strong passion. Placed round the neck at night it can bring dreams and visions and at the same time prevents the wearer from indulging in too much sleep. From the use of the amethyst an individual can become far sighted, gain understanding and become quick witted. Virtue, high ideals and lofty ideas spring from the amethyst. It contains honourable and spiritual qualities, and the wearing of this stone can help those who wish to break the fetters of vice. Through the amethyst can be obtained protection from evil influences and enemies. It makes a man vigilant, creates a clear mind and produces an atmosphere of

calm. It was considered by the ancients
that to drink a potion of amethyst the
barren would be made fruitful; it would
also expel poison. As the stone corresponding to, and is at the head of, the
Mystical and Ritual Ray its use in any
form of deep meditation would be an
asset. The amethyst should indeed have
expansive and jovial qualities as it is
always classed as being the gemstone
of Jupiter. Many occult sources also
associate it with the Archangel Adnachiel and one of its biblical associations
is with the tribe of Issachar. Gems are
used as symbols of colour in heraldry
and the colour connected with the amethyst is purpure. This is the gemstone
that many people associate with the
zodiacal sign of Aquarius, but as it is
the twelfth foundation of the new Jerusalem it is more appropriate to the
sign of Pisces. The confusion arises
because the amethyst is the gemstone
for the month of February. It can affect
the vision of the Soul and create within
it absolute reverence.

Amandinus

This is a stone of various colours
and it is credited with the power to aid
in the interpretations of dreams and
other enigmas, to solve any questions
related to them. The expulsion of poison
is also purported to be a virtue of this

stone.

Amianthus

Is rather like feathered alum, but there is quite a difference; this stone will not burn, neither is it bitter or astringent as is alum. As a talisman it is a safeguard against magicians and their evil. Resists poisons and is soothing for a skin itch; it is even supposed to cure the itch, is recommended by the ancients as a cure for menstrual troubles. Made into a liniment it can be efficacious for scalds and is also useful for ulcers (external).

Amianton and Amiatus as Amianthus

Anancithidus

According to ancient mythology by the possession and use of this stone the owner will have the power to call up evil spirits and ghosts. The author suggests that the reader does not try just in case it is not mythology.

Androdamas

Leonardus, physician to the Borgias, stated that this stone restrained anger, subdued violent emotions of the mind and mitigates the desire for luxury. It is also useful for lessening the gravity of the body.

Andromantes

This is a black stone and if it has the properties accredited to it, it should be in the working equipment of every diviner as it attracts unto itself silver, in a similar manner to the loadstone attracting iron; the andromantes is also supposed to have the same effect with brass.

Anthracites or Antrachas

Albert Magnus classifies this stone as a carbuncle because of its fiery sparkling colours. Other authorities disagree and classify it as a separate stone. It has similar properties to that of the carbuncle. One of its uses is to purify foul air. It is also supposed to keep the owner safe from harm.

Armenian Stone

So called because it was first found in Armenia but today can be found in Germany. It is frequently found in silver mines. A spotted stone in green, blue and blackish. It is, according to ancient treatise, good for mental illness, melancholy, epilepsy, and the eyes if bathed in a solution of this stone. It also has purging qualities.

Aquamarine

This stone has been called the gem of "all life", possibly because it can give visions of the future. In olden days it was part of the magicians equipment and may even be so today. In 1907 it was reported that the Earl of Denbigh, then Ambassador at Venice, stated that an aquamarine or beryl had shown him three things, past and to come. If worn as an amulet it can bring joy and exhultation; it is credited with the power to make the bearer rich and cheerful. Preserves and increases conjugal love. Hung around the neck it drives away idle dreams and prevents any disease of throat or jaw and keeps the head clear. Occultists of bygone days claimed that mixed with an equal part of silver it would cure leprosy. Water potentized by the aquamarine is good for the eyes and taken inwardly can dispel heaviness; is useful for liver complaints It is also claimed to help in the prevention of abortive births. The owner and wearer of an aquamarine will increase their receptiveness; it will also increase their powers and desires of acquisition.

The danger of this stone is its tendency to make the wearer lascivious. Apart from being called the gem of "all life" it might also be called the "elixir of life" because according to ancient teachings this gem gave everlasting youth. In the days of the Roman Empire sailors wore this stone as an amulet that was their protection against drowning.

B

Balasius

This stone is called by some people the carbuncle, but its colour is much paler. Its virtues are to control vanity, restrict the love of luxury, will aid in the reconciliation of quarrels between friends, bring good health, is good for the eyes and also for the liver. If the four corners of a house are touched with the Balasius it is supposed, according to ancient tradition, to protect the property from lightning.

Beloculus

A white stone with, as Leonardus expresses it, a black pupil. The Syrians used to put it in the ornaments of their sacrifices to the God Belus because of its beauty. It was considered, if worn around the neck, to render the owner invisible on the field of battle.

Beryl

See aquamarine which is the same stone.

Bezoar, Beza or Bezuar

The bezoar is a dusty red stone, very brittle, but in the days of the Borgia's was valued for its ability to expel any type of poison from the body. Kidney troubles are also supposed to respond to this stone, perhaps because the stone itself was found in the kidneys of wild goats.

Bloodstone

One of the chief virtues of this stone is propagation and should there- fore find a use in husbandry and the breeding of animals; it is the stone of fruitfulness. Courage, success, wisdom and riches are a few of the benefits obtained from the bloodstone and the owner of one should be fortunate. In the therapeutical field it is good for hemo- rrhoids, fevers, and is supposed to resist dropsy. If moistened and applied to wounds it is said that it will staunch the flow of blood and cure the wound. The

28

wearer of a bloodstone will find themselves becoming very popular and if
already popular, find that their popula-
rity increases. Bloodstones have been
credited with relieving arthritic pains.
It has been said that this gem will destroy
or mitigate the wrath of Kings and
Dictators. Worn against the chest it is
supposed to have the power to prevent
internal haemorrhage. The bloodstone
is of the Jasper family and, according
to legend, a piece of Jasper lay at the
foot of the Cross and the Master's blood
dripped onto it creating the red spots
from which it takes its name. As a
talisman it will guard the wearer from
deception and he will also be believed
whatever he may say. Witches of olden
days would have a bloodstone with a bat
carved on it to give her power over
demons and also to aid her in her incan-
tations. It cools and dries, is good for
eye ulcers and beneficial to the lungs.

Bronia

This stone, according to Leonardus, is like "the head of a shell". Its
only virtue is its ability to resist
lightning.

Bufonite

A cure for snake bites and of other

poisonous reptiles.

C

Carbuncle

In the dark it appears like a fiery coal. It can not be hurt by fire. There are male and female; in the male, stars appear burning within them, but the females have just their brightness throughout. Amongst its virtues is the power to drive away poisonous and infectious air, preserves the health of the body, takes away vain thoughts and represses luxury.

Used as a charm it increases prosperity and will reconcile differences amongst friends. The carbuncle was also called at one time "Anthrax". Greek sailors were very fond of this stone and had amulets or talismans made from it as a protection against drowning. It can also be used as a stimulant, particularly for the heart. The carbuncle is of the Garnet family and the Koran states that the fourth Heaven is made of carbuncle.

Carnelian

Possessed of magical power, it has been said that this was the betrothal stone of the Virgin Mary. It brings good fortune in matrimonial affairs and has the virtue of devoted love. The carnelian promotes contentment and strengthens as well as promotes friendships; disperses anger and strife, protects from evil and prevents misfortune; is an aid to the preservation of life. Fears can be expelled and courage gained by the wearer of the carnelian. It is generally supposed that the carnelian in the High Priests Breastplate had curative powers, since then it has been credited with the power to cure haemorrhoids, is useful for all forms of haemorrhage and is a defence against poisons and can make and keep fertile. Just as the carbuncle was popular with the Greeks so was the carnelian with the Egyptians and Romans, but in different ways. With the Egyptians it was used as an amulet for the dead Pharaohs and was placed in the tomb with them as a protection on their journey from this world to the next. The Romans wore them as rings to preserve the living. It was accepted that the carnelian would protect them from injury. If the ring had Serapis carved upon it, time was symbolised, and if it was Isis, it was symbolic of earth although Isis was a Moon Goddess. It may be that this is reconciled by the fact that the carnelian inspires true passion, a Moon quality at an earth level. For its wearer the carnelian secures good fortune and gives astral vision, but destroys and prevents fascination.

Cats Eye

The cat's eye is a stone that should
be worn by all who rule and politicians
could also find it very useful as it warns
of dangers and troubles. In olden times
it was used as an amulet to protect the
wearer from evil spirits and then at a
later date as a protection against witchcraft. It is a lucky stone and enriches
the wearer, but to dream of a cat's eye
symbolises treachery from friends.

Chalcedony

It should be a popular gemstone
today for those who know and believe in
the power of gemstones, because
according to Leonardus it drives away
fantastic illusions and preserves the
wearer from melancholy. It also main-
tains the vigor of the whole body, just
the gem for those engaged in the present
day rat race. Curbing lust is also a
virtue of the chalcedony, protects from
tempests and all forms of sinister
events. A stone favoured by both Romans
and Greeks, worn as a ring to bring
good fortune and to bring victory in all
forms of legal action and fills the wearer
with an ardent zeal. Worn as a talisman
it keeps the wearer healthy and protects

him on all his journeys; if worn by a sailor it preserves him from drowning. Truthfulness and faith are virtues of the chalcedony. In a powder form it will staunch the flow of blood. To wear this stone gives a cheerful mind and increases the wearer's strength. It is the eighth stone in the High Priest's Breast Plate. Its therapeutical value is to cure hoarseness and afflictions of the throat.

Chrysolite

A cure for madness and despair, it gives hope to the wearer and banishes misfortunes, relieves anxiety and worry; at the same time it gladdens the heart. Used as a talisman the wearer will not be restrained by any obstacles. Friendship, justice, wisdom and honour are all attributes of the chrysolite. It is good for legal dealings, takes away wrath, will attract marriage, ward off fevers, and cools boiling water. According to Camillus Leonardus, physician to Caesar Borgia, a potion made of chrysolite was helpful to those suffering from asthma. Worn as a charm it renders ineffectual the magic and spells of witches, drives away evil spirits and protects the wearer from folly. Worn at night it is credited with bringing sound sleep to the wearer; if worn in the daytime it is supposed to give literary and poetical inspiration. It was considered by the **ancient occultists** that the chrysolite was of a solar nature; this may be because some types of chrysolite placed under the rays of the Sun then represent golden stars. Useful for lung troubles and periodic difficulties.

Chrysoprase

Eloquence is one of the chief attributes of this gemstone. It also has the quality of severity towards sin and at the same time it was believed that if worn by a thief or placed in his mouth he could escape from his executioners. It is possible, if correct, that these two extremes could be caused through the green colour of the gem, the Green Ray being the ray of harmony through struggle and conflict. If the chrysoprase follows the ray of its colour it will be a stone of turbulence but always with an underlying harmony. A typical example of the chrysoprase Green Ray influence is that of Alexander the Great who had a chrysoprase set into his girdle as a talisman when he went into battle.

Coral

First to deal with coral irrespective of its colour. This stone was always looked upon as a protector against all evil influences and evil spirits. Coral preserves from danger. It has uses at both ends of the scale, to the high-powered business tycoon it is a tonic for the brain and for the baby it is excellent for cutting teeth. It was also accepted in the days of Leonardus that it would prevent infants from being born with epilepsy. Coral excites nerve power and it promotes brilliance. In the anatomy of Man, coral is related to the tongue. This stone has a large number of diseases that succumb to its healing vibrations:- whooping cough, croup, chronic convulsive coughs, and is a cure for acidity. It also cools down fevers, strengthens the stomach and liver and is efficacious in the treatment of the heart, lungs, and indigestion.

Red Coral is a remedy against melancholy and gladdens the heart and spirit. It is also endowed with occult sacred virtues, purifies the blood and is a cure for sterility, baffles witchcraft, counteracts poisons and protects from robbers. Red coral was also used in the time of Leonardus to stop haemorrhage of any description. Used as a talisman it preserves the wearer from illusions, bad dreams, winds, tempest and lightning. It can be found efficacious for stomach pains, the heart, spleen and intestines. Leonardus affirmed that powdered coral drunk in wine was a remedy for gravel. Powdered red coral can strengthen and restore shrinking gums and gonorrhoea will also respond

35

to red coral.

White Coral Good for ulcers, stops
weeping eyes, refreshes the sight and
will aid in the healing of scars and can
be used for abdominal colic. Plato com-
ments on coral that it has some special
sympathy with nature for the best coral,
if worn round the neck, will turn pale
if the wearer becomes ill and will return
to its normal colour as the wearer re-
covers his health.

Crisonterinus

This stone borders on a gold colour
and is very brittle. It's one virtue is to
remove the pain which children feel
when cutting teeth. It is used as an un-
polished stone.

Crystal

Worn as a talisman at night it keeps
away bad dreams and it also dissolves
spells enabling the wearer to have good
dreams and a calm sweet sleep at the
same time. The crystal enables dev-
elopment of the intuition at any time,
likewise the wearer can foretell the
future. It is probably from this ancient

belief that the crystal ball was developed. Answers to petitions and desires
can be found with the right use of and
attitude towards the crystal by its owner.
Other virtues of this gem are:- a cure
for dysentery; it is an astringent, effective in the use for colic, diarrhoea and
gout. It is also very useful for all diseases of the flesh. Held in the mouth the
crystal assuages thirst. In the Middle
Ages those who used natural remedies,
and even the occasional doctor used the
crystal for cauterising by letting the
sun's rays shine through it and so burn
the skin.

Cysteolithos

This stone has a mixture of whiteness with citron. It is found in the sea
sponge and it is not a pretty stone. It
is effective for stones in the bladder or
kidney and powdered, drunk in wine, is
good for lung troubles and bronchitis.

D

Demonius

A gemstone mixed with a double
colour and is said to expel poison, keeps
the wearer safe from his enemies and
even makes him a conqueror over them.

Diacodas or Diacodus

Rather like a beryl in colour it is a pale coloured stone. The diacodas is credited with disturbing devils more than any other gem. It was believed in the Middle Ages that if this stone was thrown into water with the words of a charm sung it showed various images of devils and would give answers to those that questioned it. If held in the mouth a man could call up the devil or any devil out of hell and receive answers to any question he may ask the devil. The diacodas is said to lose all its virtues if it touches a dead person.

Diamond

Looked upon by all men as the supreme head of the gem kingdom, also as the gem of pledged faith, love and friendship. The diamond possesses the virtue of purity, preserves peace and is supposed to prevent storms. In the Middle Ages it was used as an amulet to keep free of the devil's clutches and could perform this task day or night. It was also worn as a protection against the plague. The diamond will give way to no material thing other than another diamond. It resists all the elements and so bestows the wearer with the quality of endurance. It has been stated that a diamond bound to a magnet will prevent

38

the magnet attracting iron. Described by one ancient physician as being the finest antidote for poisons and a defence against the arts of sorcery, will disperse fears and quell quarrels, will help the mentally unstable and drive out entities from those possessed. Bound to the left arm it will give victory over enemies. Worn on either arm at night it is supposed to have the ability to cure sleeplessness and prevent bad dreams. Used correctly there is in the diamond power to tame wild beasts. In the field of gem therapy diamonds have always been classed as the gemstones for heart troubles (I would say in more ways than one) and very efficacious for gout, convulsions and delirium tremens will sometimes respond to the use of the diamond. The diamond all down the ages has brought out the avarice in man, so although in some instances it will drive away the devil, in others it is the devil's agent, and in the Kabbalistic sense it has the potential for being positive or negative and is very appropriate in its correspondence to the Tarot Card of "The Fool". Many titles have been given to the diamond, "Emblem of the Sun", "Charm of the Invisible Fire". The Greeks called it "The Holy Necessity". It is supposed to have a special relationship with the bones of man. Amongst the virtues of this gemstone are faith, joy, innocence, repentance, courage and it develops the art of concentration in the wearer. Poisons can be detected by the diamond; according to the wise men of the Middle Ages it would show a moisture on its surface at the presence of poison. Justice is another virtue, and it will promote spiritual ecstasy, maintain unity and love, drive away unreasoning fears, give hardiness to the wearer, keep the limbs whole if worn and make fearless more than careful. It will keep the wearer in good wit and will return any evil influences to the sender, exorcise ghosts and is efficacious for mental disturbance. The diamond is a protection against wild beasts and thugs. It resists acids and alkalies alike, in all it reigns supreme. The diamond is reputed to be the gemstone of the Archangel Hamatiel.

Dionysia

A black stone with red spots, as far as can be traced it has only one virtue, if it is dissolved in water it disperses drunkenness and overcomes the odour of wine and disperses it.

E

Eagle Stone
Other names: Ethices, Endes, Aquileus

The holder of mystical properties if made after the Kabbalistic art, by engraving it with the sign of an eagle and under certain stars. Scarlet in colour, it is a hollow stone with a loose kernel inside so that it rattles. This stone renders its owner amiable, sober and rich; preserves him from adverse casualties and if applied to a pregnant woman prevents miscarriage. The Eagle stone holds the virtues of the sciences and would benefit the wearer in his studies of philosophy, astronomy, physiogmony and the divination of dreams. If bound to a woman's thighs it will aid childbirth, but it must be removed immediately after the birth as it may draw the womb towards it.

Emathitis or Emathites

Similar to the Haematite stone in its virtues, but where the Haematite is black the Emathitis is of a reddish colour. It claims its name from its virtue; Emeth signifies blood and its principal virtue is to stop bleeding. Supposed to be an excellent remedy for menstrual disorders. Ground, and with the white of an egg and honey added to it, cataracts are supposed to respond to it. The dust of the Emathitis dissolved is said to cure stones in the bladder.

Emerald

Old tradition has it that if the face of the Emerald is evened it reflects images like a looking-glass. Nero Caesar was supposed to have had a very large emerald in which he beheld the combats of the gladiators. It has an astringent quality and is also useful for eye strain and a number of other eye troubles. Bound to the hip it helps childbirth. The use of the emerald for dysentery, ulcers, liver disorders and snakebites can help considerably in their cure. At the mental level it can help to dispel fears, calm the nerves and restrain anger. In the old days it was reputed by the ancients to be a deterrent for possession by elementals or discarnate spirits. Considered good for diseases of the heart and held firmly to the temple relieves headaches. It is considered efficacious for melancholy. In ancient times the emerald was used as an antidote for many different kinds of poison. It has a peculiar property that magnetically can touch the emotions so that an individual can express their indwelling and perhaps latent tenderness. In India, emeralds were used to decorate the temples and the gods because of its symbolism of true love and quality of truth. It is also a keeper of vows and anyone breaking a vow in the presence of an emerald, the gem would indicate it by losing its colour, or its sparkle would become dim. The emerald will aid either man or woman to attract a loving partner. There is an old rhyme expressing this:-

"Who first beholds the light of day"
"In Spring's sweet flowery month of May"
"And wears an emerald all her life"
"Shall be a loved and happy wife".

The Romans believed that emeralds
held supernatural powers and that they
would protect them from all evil influences. Perhaps it is the belief in this
power that it was used so much in India.
It is also a symbol of immortality and
conquers sin and trials and tribulations.
All down the ages and particularly in the
Middle Ages the emerald was claimed
to give its owner clairvoyant powers if
held under the tongue and as an amulet
was a defence against all kinds of sorcery and a protection against the powers
of darkness. In the city of Manta a very
large emerald was worshipped by the
Peruvians; it was known as Uminia, the
emerald goddess, and was only shown
to the population on feast days. King
Solomon was supposed to possess four
large emeralds from which came his
power and wisdom over all creation,
covering the four quarters of the Universe. The emerald was one of the
stones in the magical necklace of Vishnu,
the Hindu god, and was symbolic of
Earth as a magnetic centre for human
passions. Practitioners of the Middle
Ages used the emerald for stupidity and
all forms of mental illness. They also
regarded it as being good for colic. It
is reputed to blind serpents, gives courage and averts all infectious diseases,

Six to eight grains was usually the prescribed dose. Further uses of this gem was for convulsions in children, fits and it creates constancy of mind; related to the bone marrow it carbonates in the bones. Set in lead it was most efficacious for the nervous system, the brain and spinal cord. Other virtues of this all useful and powerful gem: any object of destestation and contempt becomes overwhelmed by it, discovers false friends, gives faith and also prosperity, suavity of manner, constancy of mind, success in travel and protects against all dangers in travel. A number of sources relate it to the Archangel Muriel, but with the emerald green and its varied protective powers I would be inclined to say it was the gemstone of Michael. A number of occult sources state that the chalice or Holy Grail was made from one large emerald. The closer the emerald is examined with all its various qualities and the more the green ray of harmony through struggle and conflict becomes apparent.

Enydros or Eryndros

A stone of crystal colour and takes its name from Hydros. This stone has only one use as far as can be discovered and that is for fevers and high temperatures.

Epistides or Epistrites

A glittering red stone, first found in Corinth. If fastened over the heart with magical hands and repeating proper invocations it will keep a man safe from misfortune. It drives away locusts, mischevious birds, blighting winds and storms.

Ethices or Endes

Another name for this gemstone is Aquileus. Not a well known stone but nevertheless it is credited with certain qualities. If tied to the left arm of a pregnant woman it prevents abortion, and if in the hour of birth it is bound to the thigh it removes dangers and accele-rates birth. It is a help in epilepsy and drives away poisonous creatures. Wea-rears of this stone become amiable, sober and rich, and the stone preserves them from accidents.

Eumeits

If put under the head when sleeping will produce dreams like oracles.

Exebonos or Exebenus

Restrains lechery. It is a cure for

45

mental illness and is helpful in stomach upsets, prevents miscarriage and is supposed to dissolve stones in the bladder.

Falcones

A stone very seldom heard of, but Leonardus says that it is called "one of the spirits" and that it has a warming and drying virtue. It is also claimed that if this stone is sublimated three or four times it has the power to corrode all metals except Gold. If pulverised and placed into a wound it eats away the proud flesh. Taken inwardly it is a poison to all animals.

Filaterius

Disperses terror and melancholy, soothes passions, gives cheerfulness and wisdom but can make the wearer of it complacent. It also comforts the spirits.

Fingites

Is of a white colour, hard as marble but transparent. A legend asso-

ciated with this stone:- a certain King
built a temple of this stone without
windows, but from its transparency the
light was admitted into it as though it
were full of windows.

Fongates

A red fongites carried in the hand
removes diseases of the body and ass-
auages anger.

Fricius

Dioscorides said of this stone that
it would cure fistulas and gout.

G

Galatides

Other names for this stone are
Galactica and Gelatia. Usually it is a
white lucid stone in the form of an acorn
and so cold that it is difficult to warm
it. Its coldness repels luxury and restrains anger. It can be useful as a
remedy for fevers and also for counter-
acting inflammation.

Garatronicus

Also known as the Galgatromeus,
it is a reddish stone with small saffron

veins. It has, as far as can be traced, only one virtue, that of giving victory in battle. It is reported that Achilles always carried one when he went to war. The only time he fell to his enemies was the one occasion he failed to carry his garatronicus. In olden times Eastern peoples made the hilts of their swords from the garatronicus so that they could never go into battle without it since its virtue is to render its bearer the conqueror.

Gargates

This is numbered amongst the stones, although it is in the same classification amber; as amber is a resin, gargates is gum or resin. It is a black stone, dry and opaque. If heated by rubbing it will attract straws and chaff. If burnt the smoke of it drives away devils and dissolves spells and illusions. This stone was used in the Middle Ages for dropsy. Used as a perfume it is supposed to provoke menstruation, to cure epilepsy and is a protection against the serpent or its bite.

Garnet

In the Middle Ages this stone was called Granate and it was maintained that it made the heart cheerful, drove away sorrow and protected the wearer from all pestilential disease. Both Dr. Rowlands and M. Pomet, in the 17th century, stated that the garnet was a cure for palpitations, resisted melancholy and induced sleep. The garnet was also a specific against cramp, convulsions and a cure for poisons. Many beliefs by many different nations have been handed down over the generations in connection with the garnet. Some of the Asiatic peoples used garnets for making bullets, believing that the red coloured stone could inflict a deadlier wound than bullets made of lead. In the 19th century a rebellion of Indian tribesmen, mainly Hanza, fired bullets made of garnet at the British troops. Even in England the legends of the garnet were added to in Victorian days. The first eternity rings were made of garnet, presumably because of its qualities of constancy and fidelity. Other qualities of this stone are friendship, power, grace and victory to the wearer, good health, contentment, and a safeguard from evil dreams. It is said of them that by changing colour they warn the wearer of impending danger, will guard travellers from danger and protect from lightning. Honour is one of the basic qualities of this gemstone. It was once regarded as a luminous stone that shone by night and by day. The Talmud informs us that Noha's Ark was illumined by one large but perfectly cut garnet. Common belief held that the garnet developed the psychic powers and should be worn by those desirous of seeking into the mysteries of nature. Worn as an amulet or charm it was said to confer on the wearer not only affection but constant unchanging affection with full happiness. Its curative powers were directed to any illness connected with the blood such as anaemia or low blood pressure. It stops internal haemorrhage and will dissolve tartar; will also prevent injuries being sustained.

Gerades

A red glittering stone whose only virtue is to defend the wearer from birds of prey.

Grogius

This is an alternative for coral.

Gulosus or Glosopetra

According to Leonardus this stone is like a human tongue from which it takes its name. It has been said that this stone is not formed in the Earth but in the wane of the Moon it falls from heaven and it excites the Lunar Motions.

Haematite

For a large number of blood conditions; anaemia, low blood pressure and similar troubles. It is also supposed to be a cure for mange. Where the ruby would be too strong, the Haematite could be invaluable as a tonic with many advantages over crude iron tonics, being more gentle in its work.

Hamonis

This little known stone of a gold colour is numbered amongst the most sacred gems. Found in Ethiopia it has the shape of a ram's horn. If worn or held while contemplating it gives the mind a vision of Divine things.

Heliotrope

There are diverse opinions on this stone. Some say it is a bloodstone, others believe it is a stone in its own right. As the heliotrope it makes the wearer constant, renowned and famous, gives safety and protection to the wearer protects against insect and reptile stings and ensures a long life and protects him from deceit of others. It so dazzles the eyes of man that it causes the wearer to become invisible if it has applied to it the herb bearing the same name (Heliotropium or Sunflower).

Hyacinth

This stone is found in many yellow or yellowish colours and is frequently looked upon as a jacinth. Virtues of this stone are classed as strengthening the mind, also the heart, a specific for cramp and convulsions. Worn round the neck or finger it is a protection against infection and lightning. The hyacinth is an antidote for poison and is supposed to possess virtues from the Sun which makes it a protection against pestilence and pestiforous vapours, also ruptures. It renders the wearer pleasant and acceptable. It is presumably the Sun association that gives the stone its virtues of honour and wisdom and procures for the wearer riches. Calmness in all things and the gift of second sight also come from the hyacinth.

Hyena

The use of this stone in the Middle Ages was for seeing into the future. The mouth was rinsed and the stone placed under the tongue. It was considered to be a cure for the ague and the gout.

Iona Stone

This stone has a long tradition of protecting the wearer from the dangers of drowning.

Iris

The iris is rather like a crystal in colour. It usually has six corners. When held in the shade, but letting the Sun shine through it, it represents a natural rainbow. The virtues of this stone are the same as the crystal.

J

Jacinth

This stone, according to Leonardus, is a stone of the daylight as it fades at night. It invigorates animal life. This is the stone to use for dispersing sorrow and imaginary suspicions. This means that any kind of suspicion that is not dispersed by the jacinth is in all probability correct, but if it disperses by holding the jacinth there is no truth in the suspicion. It is a stone that possesses the power to increase ingenuity, glory and riches. It is a defence against lightning and enemies, also a safeguard for travellers against any disease in any country that may hurt them. It preserves from epidemics and strengthens the heart. It was also used in the Middle Ages to prepare women for a miscarriage. Held in the mouth the jacinth strengthens the mind and either gives or increases wisdom. A good remedy for insomnia as it is supposed to induce sleep. The jacinth possesses virtues from the Sun against all forms of poison and noxious vapours. If worn regularly it renders the wearer pleasant and acceptable, gives also the quality of modesty. It is classed as being the stone of the Archangel Tsuriel.

Jade

To the Chinese this stone symbolised the five cardinal virtues; Courage, Modesty, Charity, Wisdom and Justice. It was the betrothal stone of the East. Jade brings good luck as it has fortune bestowing powers. Worn as a talisman it protects its wearer against accident, disease and witchcraft. Both Chinese and Egyptians believed that jade contained the essence of Heaven and Earth and because of this came the belief that it had the ability to confer a long life and a peaceful end. The Chinese also claimed that it preserved the corpse from decaying and so placed jade of various colourings in the nine apertures of the body before burial. It was the "Neshem" or sacred boat of the Sun God, to the ancient Egyptians. In South and Central America jade knives were used to kill human sacrifices. This same practice was carried on in Mexico. The Aztec religion, like many other religions, had its virgin birth. The Mother of their God, Quetzalcoatl, became pregnant when She swallowed a piece of jade. They also believed that if powdered and swallowed it would give them immortality.

Jade holds within it the quality of loyalty, is efficacious for kidney troubles and for stones in the bladder. Many types of nervous troubles will also yield to the calm soothing effects of jade.

Jasper

Jasper worn round the neck is supposed to be, according to ancient tradition, a protection against fevers and dropsy. It clears the sight and expels noxious phantasms. This stone is a restraint against luxury and prevents conception. Its chief virtue is to stop bleeding in any form. Other medicinal properties of this gem are that it strengthens the stomach, creates an appetite with good digestion. It is also very good for colic and epilepsy. The powder of

Jasper ground fine is an astringent, prevents formation of stones in the bladder and is a cure for haemorrhoids. Used as an amulet it is a protection against witchcraft. Worn round the neck set in gold it balances and keeps menstruation periods regular and painless. Gives to the wearer courage and wisdom, firmness, success in dangerous enterprises and gives constancy. The Jasper is also useful for the success of crops. The Aztecs laid great store by this stone because of its curative powers. It has been stated that the immortals gazed upon the jasper with pleasure. In the eyes of occult sources the bloodstone is in fact a jasper (see the legend under bloodstone) although it may be a type of jasper it is not of the species referred to under this heading. Jasper is the gem of the Archangel Barchiel which the bloodstone is not.

Jasper (red)

This form of jasper is very efficacious in stomach disorders and very beneficial for all forms of haemorrhage. The warmth from its colour vibrations also makes it useful for chest and lung troubles. It can also be used as a mild tonic.

Jet

Therapeutically this stone can be of help in dealing with flatulence, indigestion, epilepsy and temper. Worn as an amulet it gives victory over enemies.

Jews Stone

This stone is also known as Lapis Judaicus and it is shaped rather like an olive. The virtues of this stone are the curing of difficulties of urination, stones of the bladder and kidneys. It was given in a powder form. It was also used for eye strain. Another name for this stone is Cogolites.

K

Kabrates

Also known as Kakabres, it is like a crystal in colour with a cloudy whiteness. It makes the wearer eloquent of speech, gives a cheerful disposition and benevolence. Defends the wearer from accidents, brings honour and is a cure for dropsy.

Kamam or Kakaman

A white stone that is flecked with various colours and is found in hot and sulphurous places. It has no specific virtue of itself but takes its virtues from the images that are engraved upon it and is therefore an ideal stone for the making of talismans.

Kinocetus

There is only one virtue attached to this stone and it is that of casting out devils.

L

Lacteus

Citrine in colour, this stone if powdered is very useful for many forms of eye troubles.

Lapis Calminaris

Sometimes called the stony cadmia, a yellow stone that gives off a yellow fume when burnt. Ancient legend believed that this stone was found only in the mines of metals, and this may be true, but because of this it was claimed to bring riches to the wearer by guiding him to further natural stores of metals. It dries, cleanses and binds, so is useful in the healing of cuts or wounds. Cleanses and heals ulcers but must only be applied or used outwardly.

Lapis Lazuli

The Lapis Lazuli was the sapphire of the ancients and therefore this is the stone that formed the tablets on which the law was given to Moses. Accepted as one of the most useful of all stones in the field of Gem Therapy, it works at all levels of being, physical, emotional and mental. At the physical level it counteracts poisons, having great antiseptic properties, purifies the blood, relieves headaches and is useful in a number of eye troubles and is also a purgative and beneficial in diseases of the spleen. Strengthens the heart and the sight, prevents faintings and abortions, but in the case of using it to prevent abortions it must not be taken until near the time of the delivery, otherwise it may hold up the birth. At the emotional level it should be used in powder form and taken internally for melancholy, unhappiness and pride; they all yield to Lapis Lazuli. On the mental level peace of mind can be obtained and many mental disorders succumb to its properties. It has been said that through the Lapis Lazuli a man can tune in to God, perhaps this is how Moses received the law so easily and it could be this factor which gives it such healing powers over mind illness such as epilepsy and apoplexy and some forms of dementia. It gives peace of mind and has a calming influence. Used in powdered form externally it is supposed to be a cure for boils and ulcerations. With all that is credited to it by the ancients it may be worth the time and trouble to research into the properties of this gemstone. If used as an amulet and placed round the neck of a child it will drive away fears.

Lapis Linguis

Another name for this stone is Azurite. Just as the Lapis Lazuli can help man to tune in to God so the Lapis Linguis can form a link with the Astral World. It is possessed of invisible psychic links and can be an aid in developing psychic powers but should be used with care and discrimination. Is beneficial in the treatment of ulcers and enteritis.

Lapis Lyncis

Belemnites is the alternative name for this stone. It is found in the shape of an arrow or the Idean date. It is found on Mount Ida in Candy and is sometimes shaped like the mountain. It is also found round and pyramidal and is found in many differing colours. It has been said that if it be old it has a smell that nothing can remove. This apart it was used as a cure for wounds and also for pleurisy. When in the Earth, this stone is soft, but when put in a dry place it hardens. While it is kept in the Earth or moist place it generates mushrooms, and the stone or the mushrooms will help gravel or stones, take away stomach pains and cure fits. It is quite possible that this is the same stone that many centuries ago was called the Lyncurium which was made into a kind of amber.

Lauraces

These little known stones were used in the Middle Ages as a cure for headaches.

Lignites

This is a beautiful stone, crystal in colour. Hung round a child's neck it protects it from witches and witchcraft. If bound round the head it will stop the nose from bleeding and restores the unconscious. To hold a Lignite in the hand helps the holder to foretell future events.

Ligurius

Useful for stomach pains, beneficial for jaundice, and sharpens the sight, and by the physicians of the Middle Ages ranked as one of the best remedies for the eyes.

Limacie

Not a very well known stone. It is white in colour, small, like a piece of finger nail. If hung around the neck preserves the wearer from fever.

Limphicus

If wrapped in silk, this stone, according to Leonardus, preserves against all troubles of the eyes, jaws, throat, a cough or a headache, not only in the present but also in the future.

Lippares or Liparia

To this stone all kinds of animals go of their own accord by natural instinct as it is supposed to have a wonderful virtue of defending animals. The man who wears this stone will have all animals as his friends.

Lodestone

A stone that draws iron unto itself
and according to old legends, shows the
points of the compass. The Diamond and
the Lodestone disagree with each other
if ancient lore be true. The Lodestone
is said to be the mysterious bone of
Horus of the Egyptian Mysteries. It has
many virtues such as increasing the
mental powers, foretelling future events,
and serves as a love philtre. A plaster
made of burnt lodestone is good for gout.
Other therapeutical attributes are as a
cure for cramp and to stop external
bleeding. The loadstone is an astringent.
Taken inwardly it would render the
individual stupid and intoxicate him. The
antidote for intoxication by lodestone
is gold or emerald. Used as a charm it
reconciles husbands to wives or vice
versa. It makes a man gracious. If held
in the hand by the mother to be it helps
childbirth. Taken in powder form in
honey it cures dropsy by purging. Taken
with the juice of fennel it is good for
troubles of the spleen. If the head is
rubbed with it it cures baldness. According to Leonardus this stone has the
power to discover adulterous wives. If
put under the head of the sleeping wife,
if adulterous she will immediately jump
out of bed and flee. Carried about it
takes away fears and jealousies and
makes a man persuasive and fine con-
versationalist. The stone exercises

influences for good or ill on any person
wearing it or being within its sphere of
radiation.

M

Malachite

A peculiar aspect of this stone is
its special association with children. In
olden times it was believed that hung
around the neck of a child or infant it
would defend it from accidents and if
hung on the cradle it would prevent
dreams and fantasies so that the infant
may grow up in prosperity. It is supposed to be efficacious for rheumatism
and cholera and prevent nightmares and
depression. It can be useful in the treatment of those who suffer from delusions.
It is the Mafkat of Syria.

Marchasites

In the Middle Ages this stone was
called the stone of light because it gave
relief to lost sight, and because when it
was struck with steel it made fire and
with the right material would kindle fire.

Medus or Medinus

The two names indicate the two
colours of the same stone, Medus
(black), Medinus (green), Leonardus

informs us that if the Medus is put into a green mortar and dissolved with the milk of a woman who has a male child and applied to the eyes it restores lost sight, but if dissolved in the milk of a ewe it cures gout if bound to the place that is affected. If taken internally it is a pernicious poison. Because of this it was called the "Giver of Death and of Health". Medinus powdered and mixed with gall, a little of the lodestone and rainwater and then put on the eyes for seven days strengthens the sight and sharpens it so that the most minute and near invisible can be seen clearly.

Melites or Melitites

When powdered in water it gives a sweet taste and is useful in many disorders of the stomach.

Memphitis

Called after the city where it was first found. Classed in the Middle Ages as a good anasthetic as its virtue is more stupifying than opium; if powdered and taken in an intoxicant or vinegar and applied to the area of the surgeon's knife, it makes that part of the body so insensible that hardly any pain can be felt.

Mirites

In both colour and smell it is like Myrrh. If rubbed on a cloth it gives out the odour of spikenard with its sweetness.

Moonstone

The Moonstone is the sacred stone of the Orient. It glitters in the dark and its brightness contains the figure of the moon or a clouded star. It was reputed to keep the times of the lunar motion and its colour to increase and decrease with the waxing and waning of the Moon. Powerful in reconciling love. During the period of the waxing moon it helps the physical but when it is on the wane it works on the psychic level. It enables a person to see into the future and forecast future events. If placed in the mouth it helps to deal with the person's affairs by fixing in the mind those things that should be done and dismissing those that should not. Apart from its occult and magical power there are therapeutic values attached to the moonstone. It is cooling in a fever if applied to both temples and is good for burns and stubborn ulcers. Worn as a charm it brings good fortune in love matters, protects from harm and danger, makes the wearer constant, renowned and famous. It also bestows long life, victory in life's battles and bestows upon its wearer great wisdom. Beneficial in treatment of cancer, dropsy and illness of a watery nature. Pope Leo X was said to possess a wonderful specimen which was obscure and dull when the moon was old, increased in brilliance as that orb grew new to old.

Murina

A stone of many colours, there is a kind of reflection of one on the other rather like the effect of a rainbow. It has been thought, according to Leonardus, that it is generated from the moisture of the earth and condensed by the heat of the sun. The therapeutical values are the same as the opal.

N

Nephrite

Invaluable in the treatment of all kidney diseases, useful for eye-sore; it also promotes childbirth, expels gravel and cures pains of the stomach. It can also be used for strengthening the veins.

Nicolus

A stone of a double colour. Outside it is yellow and inside it is black. Its virtue is to render the bearer victorious.

O

Obtalius or Obtalmius

This stone is found in many colours. Its virtue is in preserving the eyes from many eye diseases. It is said of this stone that it sharpens the sight of those wearing it but dims those of the bystanders.

Oculis Solis or Eye of the Sun

According to Francis Barrett this stone gives forth a ray which is beneficial to the brain and in Barrett's words, strengthens sight.

Olivine

Frees the mind from sadness and evil passions.

Onicinus

Though this is formed from the gum of its own tree, like amber it is classed under the gemstones. Its colour is white mixed with a moderate red. If put on a live coal, like incense it gives a sweet and fragrant smell. Cleanses the hands and cures irritations of the skin.

Onyx

The onyx is a mixture of good and bad and looked upon by many as a malefic. To anyone wearing it it stirs up quarrels and attracts many horrible things in sleep. It can also be the cause of melancholy. This turbulent gem can, however, be worn if a sardius is worn with it as the sardius can completely neutralise the mischevious influence of the onyx. Therapeutically it can be used for epilepsy, strengthens weak eyes and increases vitality. It can give a feeling of exhilaration, stimulates the spleen and holds the quality of conjugal felicity. Worn with a sardius it can protect from evil influences.

Eliphas Levi in his writings informs us that Saturday was the day for works of mourning and included in the ceremonial dress of the operator was an onyx ring on which Janus had been engraved double faced, while the planet

Saturn was in the ascendant. Saturn is the planet of the Black Ray and as such the black onyx would be one of the stones coming under Saturn's rule. Tribesmen of Burma used the onyx as a fetish stone and sacrifices were made to it, thinking that if they did not give blood to the stone for food it would eat them. The tribesmen thought that the onyx contained spirits which had to be served so that they would not cause trouble for the tribe.

Emblematic of true friendship and good health, but at the same time can cause mental heaviness and stupor, also despondency. It is the gem of the Archangel Gabriel.

Opal

As expressed by the ancients this is the stone of hope, innocence, faith, purity and achievement. If the qualities it has been endowed with are all there the ancients probably had something. Useful in treating all eye diseases, it may also be used for some mental disturbances and this in itself shows the wide embracing power of the opal as it works with great efficiency on the emotional level being beneficial in cases of anger and hate. It can imbue a feeling of love or friendship where hate previously existed. It may be because of this power to harmonise that it can be very effective where the cause of disease is rebel cells. What is there in the opal that gives it these powers? The opal contains the vibrations of all the cosmic rays. Pliny describes it perfectly when in his works he expressed the opal in the following way: The fire of the ruby, the brilliant purple of the amethyst, the sea-green of the emerald, all shining together in union. We might add to that the glinting Orange Ray, the blue of Love and Wisdom, even the pearly blue of the moonstone, all can be found in this most beautiful of the gemstones. It is, however, because of containing all these cosmic rays that the opal became maligned as an unlucky stone and the stone of the evil eye. The opal is not an evil or unlucky stone. It is in harmony with the cosmos, which the majority of mankind are not. If man can not balance the Rays within himself he can not be in harmony with the opal, but why blame the opal for man's own deficiency. A few more qualities of this lovely gem: it can strengthen the heart, prevent infection, and worn as a talisman take away the worries and cares of its wearer dispelling all melancholy. The opal was held in high esteem by the Greeks and the Romans. Nonius, a Roman senator, was exiled because he refused to sell a large opal that he owned to Mark Anthony who wanted to present it to Cleopatra. It holds and can bestow the gift of prophesy

71

and foresight. if used wrongly for selfish gain it can be unlucky for love and desires. As a charm it gives beauty to the wearer, success in warfare, contests and in handling medicine. Should be worn if following dangerous pursuits.

Opal (Mexican Fire)

Contains the soul of truth. The soul of Fire. The stone of hermits and gods who live alone. Its qualities are a vision of an ideal world, a world of far horizons. Repellent and unlucky to those who are not prepared to sacrifice the personal for the ideal.

Ostiogolla

White or ash coloured, like a bone and grows by the sand, it was used in olden times to glue bones, as one of them stated, quickly. It yields a matter to form a callus and hasten glutination.

Ostracites

This stone is rather like an oyster shell and was in the Middle Ages used as a pumice to smooth the skin. Therapeutically it was used to stop bleeding and powdered in honey it was given to assuage pains in the breasts.

Panthera

This stone comes in various colours in the one stone, but is not translucent like the opal. It is stated that if you look on it by the rising sun you will be successful in all your actions on that day. It is said that the panthera has as many virtues as it has colours and as the rays are cosmic forces this is in all probability true.

Pavonius

Is a stone which if given in a drink that is warm forces the person who takes it into a ferment of love.

Peantes

A stone described by ancient tradition as having the female sex. At a certain time it conceives and brings forth one like itself. Leonardus, however, construes the "female sex" to mean that it affords help to women at the time of conception, pregnancy and giving birth.

Pearl

This is a much used stone in the symbology of the Bible and those who are prepared to look into the many quotations and resolve their deeper meanings will understand the full potential of the pearl. Back in time people maintained that the pearl had an attunement to healing forces, creative vibrations and celestial knowledge. The white pearl for idealism, the pink for beauty and the black for philosophy. The Aztecs used the pearl for its curative power as well as the jasper. Purity and innocence are always associated with the pearl just as wisdom is always quoted as one of its virtues. It may be that this is the reason why some people cannot wear pearls, so full of innocence and beauty that they lose their brightness on a person whose purity and innocence is doubtful. If a person is in tune with the pearl and can wear one the wearer will find that all restrictions, frustrations and bad luck can be turned to advantage. Through it they can make conquests and they can triumph over the slings and arrows of outrageous fortune. In the therapeutical field excellent results are obtained at the mental level. Negative mental vibrations can be transmuted so that the untruthful can become truthful, the immoral become moral and other negative qualities can be reversed into positive qualities. At the physical level pearls give strength, are beneficial for ulcers, and stomach disorders will respond to the pearl. It can also be used for epilepsy. Worn as an amulet it wards off evil. Native divers who obtain the pearl oysters claim it gives them protection against the sharks. The Romans wore them in the belief that they would increase their wealth. Hindus say the pearl increases their virility. Other traditions have the faith that it preserves the body from old age and decay. Pearl preserves the teeth, strengthens the heart, is helpful for T.B., good for nerves, gives a clearness to physical and mental sight and is therefore a cure for mental troubles. Will act as a repellent of smallpox, can clear acid indigestion that is obstinate, will control fevers and bleeding, resists poisons and infections, strengthens the balsam of life and regulates and normalises menstruation. If Dr. Bhattacharyya M.A. Ph.D., is correct and the pearl releases orange rays, then there are many more diseases that the pearl will be a cure for. In Chromotherapy or colour healing the Orange Ray is used for such types of illness as bronchitis, mental debility, asthma, rheumatism, arthritis, phlegmatic fevers, colds, chest complaints and many others that need the warmth of this thermal ray. The Chinese valued this gem and the Taoists were of the opinion that pearls had the power to give them long life and immortality. Albertus Magnus claimed that pearls would cure haemorrhage, dysentry and affections of the heart. Aristotle was of the opinion that pearls were blood purifiers, a cure for melancholia and love sickness. Today it is the diamond that cures a woman's melancholia, but at a different level of consciousness. Pearls come in different colours; white, pink and black have already been mentioned, to this Kozminsky in his book on gems adds golden pearls as emblems of wealth, red for health and energy and the grey pearl for thought.

Peridot

A delicate coloured stone that has the virtues to clear the mind, prevent irritability and remove depression. This stone is considered by some authorities to be the topaz of the biblical days and to be a protection against demons.

Phrigius

It has the virtue of being stiptic, cures proud flesh in wounds and is useful in the treatment of malignant ulcers and inflammation of the eyes.

Pontica

A translucent blue gem sprinkled with red stars. It was said of it in olden times that by if the Devil was interrogated and put to flight and is compelled to give answers to anyone that asks him any questions.

Prassius

Called after the herb of the same name because of its similarity of colour. It is good for the sight and has similar virtues to the emerald.

Pumex or Punicus

Full of caverns, porus and easily powdered. The pumex cools, dries, extenuates, cleanses ulcers and the powder dissolved can be used as a medicine for the eyes and prevents drunkeness if taken before drinking wine.

Pyrites

Sometimes called the fire stone because when struck with steel it flashes fire. According to Leonardus it is a yellow stone. Dioscorides calls it the colour of brass. A very blunt thick stone, but finely polished by the washing of the sea. If ground and held hard between the fingers it will burn them. It was used to make a medicine for the eyes.

Q

Quartz

Many of the gemstones are of the quartz family but speaking of just quartz, under this heading is meant the white quartz. This stone holds many mysteries. Through its vibrations a man should be able to tune into the vibrations of the Universe both past and present. It has been suggested that the Urim and Thummim of the High Priest's breast plate were quartz. They glowed brightly when God was pleased and went dull when He was displeased; this being so, quartz could be a cosmic radio. It is also supposed to be a cure for dropsy.

Quirinus

Not a very well known stone but in the Middle Ages it was believed that if it was laid on the breast of a sleeping person it forced him to discover his evil side.

Radaim

A translucent black stone that if used as an amulet gives favours and honours and is of help in governing.

Ranius or Rabri or Rami

All these names apply to the same stone. Described by Leonardus it is a livid colour and borders upon white with a clearness. It has one virtue, that of resisting poisons.

Rock Crystal

Like the quartz this stone is supposed to be a link in communications between man and God. It can be used for cauterizing by directing the Sun's rays through it onto the part of the anatomy where cauterizing is required.

Ruby

This stone is also supposed to have Divine power and will banish many forms of sin and vice. Will give warning to its wearer if any evil is about or going to befall the wearer by going dark and cloudy. To anyone who is sensitive the ruby would through wearing it exercise upon them occult and physical magnetic action. Worn as an amulet it drives away evil spirits, protects the wearer from war injuries, restrains lust and cleanses the mind of evil thoughts and protects from horrible and frightening dreams. The ruby amulet will ensure that the owner will never lose rank or property and would be protected from all perils. The reason for rubies being worn on the forehead in India is because of the belief that they influence the mind; also, either fastened to the brow or placed under the pillow will give peaceful and pleasant dreams. The ruby, of course, is on the Red Ray and can influence for evil as well as good according to the character and disposition of the wearer. The ruby is closely related to the bloodstream and is very beneficial if used for anaemia, leukaemia and other diseases of the blood and circulatory deficiencies as it quickens the blood and gives vitality to the body. Other qualities of the ruby are love, dignity, loyalty, charity, success and thoughtfulness for those less fortunate than themselves. It also makes the wearer more cheerful. If the four corners of a house are touched with the ruby the house will be preserved from lightning and tempests. The ruby symbolises true friendship and if made a gift of one the receiver will have success in whatever he does. Used as a charm the owner will be free from worries, fear and misfortune, discover and resist poisons, cause obstacles to melt away, inspires courage and zeal and increases the will power. The ruby cures evil that springs from friendship or love, protects in hazardous risks and brings success in love matters. Drives away melancholy and sadness and banishes idle and foolish thoughts. It is excellent for pleasure, good for gamblers. It is also useful for creating harmonious relations with children, restores lost strength and banishes vanity and depression. From the therapeutical side of the ruby it will disperse infections, protect from the plague and can be useful in the treatment of liver disorders, lassitude, paralysis, weak muscles, poliomyelitis, oedema, moles, infantile paralysis, colds, tuberculosis and may also help to retard old age. A ruby set in iron in the form of a pentagram was used in ancient Egyptian magic. In India it was used as an aid to telepathy and for the purpose of healing. The ruby is the gemstone of the Archangel Malchidiel. Rubies grow in a stony matrix; at first they are white and by degrees ripen to red. They are commonly found in the same mine as the sapphire.

Samius

A white brittle stone with the virtues to cure vertigo, prevent abortion and restore the loss of understanding. Can help eye disorders if powdered in milk and applied to them.

Samothracia

A black coloured stone something like burnt wood and it takes its name from the place where it was first discovered. When put on a fire it smells like pitch and the fumes are useful for fits of the Mother.

Sandastros or Sadasius

There are male and female to this species. The female is a mild flame colour and the male is yellower. Both are sprinkled with gold drops which seem like stars and shine from within. There are no therapeutical values attached to this stone but it was used for its esoteric value in the ceremonies of the Chaldeans.

Sapphire

The stone of sacred occult powers. Will open barred doors and produce a desire for prayer and creates in the wearer, who must lead a pure and holy life, heavenly and beautiful thoughts. It confirms the soul in good works, is of great service in the magical arts and is said to be of great efficacy in the works of necromancy, frees from enchantments, frees the mind, dispels evil thoughts. Probably because the sapphire is for the chaste and pure it was chosen as the stone for the Cardinal's ring. The star sapphire, known as the stone of destiny, was at one time worn as an amulet by kings as a protection against enemies. The sapphire will warn its wearer of hidden dangers. It is potent in its magnetic action, giving the mind illumination through opening up the intuition. This stone vibrates purity, constancy, truth, virtue, chastity and continence. It produces peace of mind, mends manners and creates piety and goodness. By correct use of the sapphire fear and envy can be expelled from the mind and the wearer can be made amiable and kindly disposed towards his fellow beings. In the Middle Ages it was used as a testing stone for married women. If it lost its colour while being worn it indicated the wife's infidelity. Therapeutically the sapphire has many powers; most eye afflictions respond to the sapphire, excess perspiration can be checked, skin diseases respond to its treatment, all forms of inflammation, haemorrhoids and other forms of bleeding can be satisfactorily dealt with. It is a protection against smallpox and can cure internal ulcers, strengthens the heart, establish a healthy circulation and purifies the blood. Through this action it also becomes a cure for and counteracts poisons of all kinds including snake bites and scorpion stings. Dysentry, tumours not too far gone and carbuncles all respond to the power of the sapphire. All diseases of the heart, fevers, even of a malignant nature, boils and abscesses will yield to the treatment of a sapphire. It is an astringent, good for wounds even of an internal nature and a whole sapphire laid on the forehead will stop bleeding from the nose. It was even an enemy to the plague. Melancholy disperses before its powers and it removes all shadows. Purely at a material level, for which the sapphire is little known, it can be of great help in financial matters and can prosper transactions and enterprises. The sapphire symbolises repentence and its Archangel is Verchiel.

Sarcophagus

Yes, this is a stone and took its name from its effect. Sarcos in Greek

Signifies flesh, Fagos to eat, hence sarcophagus, or devouring bodies in a coffin. If this stone is bound to a man while he is alive it has the force to eat away his flesh. It was from this that all stone sepulchers became known as Sarcophaga.

Sardius or Sarda

Is or was classed as one of the burning gems. It is of a red or bloody colour but is darker and duller than a cornelian. It was first found in Sardinia from whence it took its name. It protects against horrid dreams, increases wealth, gives cheerfulness, sharpens the wit and gives conquest over enemies. Leonardus states that those who think the sardius is a cornelian are suffering from a false notion. This stone is a useful asset in the treatment of enteritis. It enobles the love principle in its manifestions.

Sardonyx or Sard or Sardonius
(also Oriental Carnelian)

Gives conjugal felicity, favours fortune and prevents misfortune. The person whose stone it is and does not wear it is doomed to a lonely existence. This stone was highly valued by the Romans. Its virtue is to put a restraint on lascivious motions and make a man merry and agreeable and averts melancholy. It is a symbol of conjugal happiness. The stone was worn as a protection against the plague and also to ward off stings and bites of poisonous insects and reptiles. It was supposed to be lucky if used in the breeding of small animals and poultry. Therapeutically it is a cure for tumours, useful in the healing of wounds providing the wound is not made by iron. The flesh coloured sardonyx was used as a styptic and to arrest bleeding of the nose. It is also a giver of spiritual strength and peace of mind. It helps to restrain temper. It sometimes consists of three layers; bottom layer black for humility; centre layer white for virtue; top layer red or brown for fearlessness; the whole stone for self-control and conjugal happiness.

Selenites, Sirites or Siderites

Virtues of this stone are found under the moonstone. The siderites branch of this stone if used in sorceries excites discord. Powdered it will stop haemorrhage.

Serpentine or Ophite

Gives the power to see visions and hear the voices of the invisible. Good for

headaches if bound on to the head. Counteracts the stings of serpents. The soft
white serpentine with lines running
through it was used as a cure for
lethargy and smallpox. Other forms of
serpentine are useful for colic pleurisy,
gripes, chill on the stomach, gout and
tuberculosis and afflictions of the
bladder.

Snakestone or Serpent Stone

Light in colour with white spots,
invulnerable to snake bites and a
supposed cure for lunacy.

Solis Gemma

The jewel of the sun, it is of a
bright white colour and when placed in
the full blaze of the sun it sends out and
spreads about its shining rays. It has a
wonderful efficacy against deadly poisons.

Specular Stone

A branch of the selenite group,
crystal, bright and flaky. The virtue of
this stone in the Middle Ages was to
beautify women and take away wrinkles.

Spinel

Preserves from lightning and restrains passions and temper. A solution of this stone is beneficial to all forms of irritation and inflammation. It can also be used for brain anaemia as it is more gentle in action than the ruby. Various forms of depression will yield to its gentle persuasion.

Stuxites

This is the ancient sex stone; hung round the neck it is good for the digestion, but also creates a desire for fruition. When powdered and taken with ragwort gives a stiffness to the penis.

Sunstone

Gives cheerfulness to the wearer, heightens spiritual awareness and energises.

T

Talc Alchimicus

A lucid luminous stone of a silver colour and is reputed to be the worst of poisons.

Thirsitis

In appearance is similar to coral. If it is liquified it is supposed to induce sleep.

Tigers Eye

A reputedly lucky stone that enriches the wearer.

Toadstone

An antidote to poisons, soothes inflammation of bee stings and other insects.

Topaz

The stone of friendship and fidelity, also of love, joy and peace. Prevents bad dreams, expels fears and protects against sorcery and magic. The ancients of the East believed that by the topaz they were able to communicate with the astral plane. For those near the end of a physical incarnation it can banish the fear of death and so make the departure easier. The topaz magnetically affects the mind; at the higher level of understanding it creates an apprehension of the wisdom of Divine love as well as wisdom in general. At the lower level of the mind it helps it to a condition of peace. With this quality it is useful in dealing with hysteria, anger and to dispel fears of any kind.

Mental conditions or many of them will disperse through the use of the topaz and it is very useful in dealing with nervous breakdowns. Remarkable cures from plague sores were claimed and ground topaz was very much in use in the Middle Ages. Powdered topaz could be purchased by the ounce in the apothecaries shops.

Topaz powdered and taken in wine was believed to cure asthma, insomnia and many other maladies. A topaz was placed in wine and left for three or four days could then be rubbed on the eyeballs and it strengthened the sight.

Worn as a talisman it is reputed to protect the wearer from the perils of the sea, indicate poisons by losing its colour in their presence, cheers the wearer and strengthens their intellect, sharpens the wit, strengthens the nerves and cures cowardice.

It should always be used by those travelling abroad and or dealing with people overseas. Useful as a cure for epilepsy and it helps the heart and is good for the digestion. Reduced to powder and mixed with rose water and taken internally to stop bleeding. Topaz is also useful for the emotions as it allays grief and gives joy.

The ancients believed that the topaz increased and decreased with the

Moon's phases. It may have been this idea that gave them the link with the mind. Also from this connection with the moon probably came the belief that topaz set in a solver ring, silver being the metal of the moon, acted not only as a tonic but gave a greater arterial blood circulation. It is also supposed to stop bleeding and by this virtue is efficacious in the treatment of piles. A German writer of the 17th century stated that when thrown into boiling water the topaz would deprive the water of its heat at once.

The Archangel to take the topaz as his stone is Ashmodei.

Tourmaline

It might be termed the cleanser. Tourmaline cleanses the internal system, is a laxative and good for skin troubles and for the teeth and bones.

Turchion or Turchesia

A yellow stone that is very pleasing to the sight. Reputed to be useful to horsemen; as long as the rider had it with him his horse would never tire him and would preserve him unhurt from any accident. Strengthens the sight and worn as a talisman it is said to defend the wearer from outward and evil casualties.

Turquoise

This gemstone has always been associated with curious superstitions. It is so sympathetic that it grows pale when its wearer is sick or loses its colour altogether at its owner's death but will recover when placed on the finger of a new owner. It was recorded in 1620 that anyone wearing a turquoise so that it touched the skin could fall from any height and the stone will attract to itself the whole force of the blow so that it cracks but the wearer remains unhurt.

If a turquoise turns green upon any person they ought not to wear it; if they do, misfortune will befall them since under such conditions the turquoise is malevolent.

If this stone is given to anyone by a loving hand it will carry with it good health, good fortune and a great deal of happiness. Worn by horsemen the turquoise is said to endow the mount with sure-footedness. It was also used in the Middle Ages as a weather guide. If the stone remained a brilliant blue the weather would be dry and a clear sky, but if its colour dimmed it was a sign of bad weather ahead.

The turquoise is always classed as the stone of prosperity and soul-cheerer, driving away melancholy. Therapeutically it is good for the eyes, some forms of insomnia, the cure and prevention for vomiting. It is excellent for any illness where the root cause is a guilt complex; a cure for headaches and an effective antidote for the stings of scorpions and insect bites.

Worn as an amulet the turquoise protects from evil spirits, drives away witches and preserves the wearer from all kinds of evil influences and also makes him lucky in love.

U

Unicorn or Ceratites

Sometimes called fossile ivory or horn because it is the colour and smoothness of horn. It is commonly hard outside but soft within.

Considered as a cure for gonorrhea, whites, nose bleeding and haemorrhoids. If it has a good scent it will strengthen the heart and cure epilepsy. Used outwardly it cures ulcers.

Urim and Thumim

No-one knows just what these magical stones were, or anything about them other than they were used for communication between the High Priest and God.

Varach

Has the virtue to stop all forms of bleeding.

Vernix .

Is said to give help to melancholia, spleen troubles, colic and liver troubles.

Vulturis

Gives health to the wearer, success to those who petition for favours and, according to Leonardus, fills a woman's breasts with milk.

Y

Yorinus

In the Middle Ages there was much dissension concerning this stone; some said it was the serpentine, others that it was a different species. Amongst those who classed it as a different species was Leonardus.

Reputed to be a cure for rheumatism, dropsy, drives away poisonous worms and if taken inwardly is said to dissolve stones in the bladder. It must be used with care, otherwise it may extract from the body the natural juices or oils.

Zarites

A stone the colour of crystal that if hung about the neck will stop bleeding.

Ziazaa

A multicoloured stone that will make the wearer see terrible things in his sleep, a stone therefore, to be avoided.

Zircon or Jargon

The stone of independence or self dependence. Is one of the species in the hyacinth and jacinth group. The zircon's value lies more in its use as a charm or amulet than as a medicine.

Worn as a charm it is a protector from wounds and injuries. Reputed to have achieved cures from the plague and is a remedy for insomnia. It was a popular charm or amulet with travellers, protecting them even from lightning.

As a heart stimulant it is thought

to be very effective and it also prevents
any form of evil dreams.

Zoronysias

Said to be found in the river Indus
and to be the stone of the Magi.
What better gem and note could
there be on which to finish this alphabe-
tical list of stones.

Preparation of Stones for
Therapeutical Use

It was maintained by Schroder that stones are made of the "Salt Terrestial Perittoma" which abounds for the nourishing of things.

The operations or preparations by which stones are made medicinal are chiefly as follows:-

(1) Powdering
(2) Calcination
(3) Solution, Coagulation and Purification
(4) Liquation
(5) Distillation or Volatilization
(6) Syrupization.

(1) Powdering or Pulverisation

Stones are best powdered by grinding first and then by pulverising, sprinkling with water whilst pulverising, so bringing the final powder to a pulp and then drying, in the sun whenever possible.

If it is desired to give the dose by grain, which in some cases may be desirable, extract so much after the grinding process and before commencing the pulverisation.

(2) Calcination

This form of preparation can be carried out in any one of three different ways, (a) simple ignition, (b) Restinct ignition or (c) Corrosion.

The simple ignition process is where a stone is burnt in the bare fire until it becomes a calx, the same method as lime burning. In the restinct ignition method the stone is fired and quenched in water alternately frequently until it is brought to a calx. With the corrosion method the stone is burnt with a treble quantity of sulphur three or four times, perhaps more, according to the stone being calcinated. This is done in an open crucible over a fire until the sulphur exhales. Sulphur is the best medium to use, but flower of brimstone could be used as an alternative.

(3) Solution

Where it is required that the calcinated stone be turned into a solution or dissolved it should be placed in a hot solution of either distilled vinegar, or juice of citrons, but chiefly the distilled vinegar. This process is repeated until the stone is nearly dissolved or will dissolve no further

There are a considerable number of liquors suggested by Schroder for dissolving stones including the use of

juice of barberries, melons and betula.
Schroder also recommends spirit of
honey, spirits of salt and turpentine.
Vinegar and juice of citrons are by far
the most suitable.

If coagulation is required, this is
achieved by the precipitation of the solution. Precipitation can be carried out
by instillation of common salt dissolved
or by oil of tartar. An alternative method
of separation is by evaporation and is
an excellent method, after evaporation
has taken place a little brandy should be
added to the remaining juice of the stone
as a preservative.

(4) Liquidation

This method is a much slower
method, but in the end a more satisfactory one. The calcined stone is placed
in a glass and left in a moist place where
it will gradually turn into liquid.

(5) Volatilisation

This is done by dissolving salt and
adding distilled water and placed in a
retort with the calcined stone. Distillation then takes place for as long as is
required. After each distillation some
common salt will ascend.

It is better to keep the essence of
the wine joined with the liquor of the salt

as they perfect each other. The resolving force of the salt is exalted by the strength of the wine essence and this in turn is made more piercing and stronger to dissolve the calcined stone.

The volatilising essence can be extracted after the stone has been dissolved by a gentle heat that will leave the essence of the stone in the bottom of the retort.

(6) Syrupisation

If it is desired to make the essence of the stone into a syrup add the juice of citrons with sugar and water until the right consistancy is achieved.

Never be afraid of weakening the essence. With this form of treatment the weaker the essence the greater the penetrating power. Care should be exercised, however, with certain stones that they are not too penetrative. The two stones that need the greatest care are the ruby and the emerald.

It should always be remembered that the small bottle of essence produced is a stock bottle and that for use two or three drops should be placed into another bottle and this filled with boiled water. The number of drops used for the medicine bottle will depend on the strength of the remedy that is required.

Before detailing the method Leonardus used in his preparation of stones, it is appropriate to mention at this point that Anselm Boetius wrote a treatise on precious stones. Boetius was the physician to Rudolphus II.

Conradus in his Destil, part 1, tract 20, also wrote a whole treatise on precious stones and other stones, their preparation and faculties.

Camillus Leonardus had many methods for the therapeutic use of stones which was not dependant on the stone, but on the nature of the specific trouble that it was required for.

The amethyst, which Leonardus used to prevent or cure drunkenness, would be bound to the navel of the individual in need of that treatment. As a cure for sterility he made it into a lotion or medicine. To safeguard military men from harm Leonardus would prescribe an amethyst to be suitably engraved and worn.

There are many diverse ways in which Leonardus used the lodestone. People suffering from cramp and gout were recommended to carry a lodestone in their clothing, but to facilitate the birth of a child the mother-to-be had to hold one in her hand.

For dropsy Leonardus suggested crushed lodestone taken with honey, but for spleen troubles the crushed stone had to be mixed with the juice of fennel. This same preparation rubbed on the head was, according to Leonardus, a cure for baldness.

Placed under the pillow of a sleeping wife would tell the husband if she
were faithful or adulterous. If faithful
she would embrace him, but if not she
would immediately jump out of bed.

It will be seen from the foregoing
that the stones had many uses and were
used for many and varied troubles other
than physical and/or mental illness.

The sapphire crushed and given in
milk was supposed to be a cure for
gripes, but to strengthen the eyes the
stone itself was gently applied to them.
This was also the method for the cure
of a headache.

Solarisation

This is one of the most satisfactory
methods of preparing medicines from
stones. Unfortunately the English cli-
mate does not lend itself too well for
this method.

After deciding which stone is
required, it is placed in a bottle of, if
available, fresh spring water. Alter-
natively boiled water should be used. It
should then be exposed to the sunlight
for twentyfour hours. Between periods
of sunlight it should be placed in a dark
cupboard.

When exposed to sunlight it should
be allowed to absorb both long and short
rays. If it is possible to carry a large
stock of the various types of stones the

maximum advantage of sunny days should be taken and as many preparations made up as it is possible to do so.

When the period of exposure is completed add a little brandy as a preservative and store in the dark cupboard. These bottles should then be used as stock bottles. From a 2 dr stock bottle, six 2 dr bottles of remedy can be prepared.

Where it is not possible, financially or otherwise to carry a large varied stock of remedies, two further methods of preparing remedies can be used, boiling or dark absorption.

Boiling Method

Place the required stone in a closed receptacle filled with water. This should be carefully measured into the receptacle and not just filled haphazardly. Each half gallon should be boiled until there is only sufficient to fill the 2 dr stock bottle.

This method of preparation is more costly than solarisation due to the stones dissolving or disintegrating more quickly, but in England probably the most certain and satisfactory, as so rarely can a twentyfour hour or two consecutive days of sunshine be guaranteed.

Dark Absorption

This is the most economical method of preparing a stone remedy, providing there is no urgent need for the remedy. The stone is placed in a stock bottle which is filled with boiled water and placed in a dark cupboard, where it must remain for at least forty-eight hours, allowing the vibrations of the stone to be absorbed into the water. Stock and preparation bottles with this method can be of any size, the careful measurement has to be applied when making up the remedy. Standard 2 dr bottles are recommended for use by the patient. This size of bottle should be half or two thirds filled with the remedy from the stock bottle, according to the strength required, and then filled with brandy.

The usual dose for a patient is two small drops, further diluted by being placed in a tablespoonful of water. The number of doses per day is left to the discretion of the practitioner. If the dose is three times per day the 2 dr bottle should last approximately four weeks.

A practitioner will know from the dose he prescribes whether the bottle of remedy will last the patient three, four, or five weeks, and should have the next bottle of remedy required ready so that continuity of treatment is not broken. This is very important.

Myths and Legends Etc.

There are many myths and legends connected with the gem stones, two of which were mentioned in the opening chapter. Those that are now to follow will give the reader a greater appreciation of the awe and esteem in which they have been held all down the centuries.

It could be construed that when Plato stated the gem stones originated in the stars, he was referring to the fifth state of matter, the Etheric.

The magic necklace of Vishnu was reputed to be made of five precious stones, each symbolising one of the five elements, pearl, ruby, emerald, sapphire and diamond-or water, fire, earth air and ether.

There is a legend contained in one of the ancient Indian works, the epic poem of the Ramayana. In the Rama Ravana war the demi-god and royal hero Maha Bali is slain, and Indra, the Lord of the atmosphere, took Maha Bali's body and with lightning cut it into many parts. From the purity of Bali's actions the different portions of his body became the germs of various gems. From his bones came diamonds; from his eyes sapphires; from his blood rubies; from his marrow emeralds; from his flesh crystals; from his tongue coral; and from his teeth pearls.

One of the ancient writers, Dioscorides, mentions the famous stone of Memphis as a small pebble, round, polished and very sparkling. When ground into powder and applied as an ointment to that part of the body on which the surgeon was about to operate, either with his scalpel or fire, it preserved that part, and only that part from any pain in the operation.

Dinocrates, a celebrated architect in the time of Alexander the Great, was induced, because of its magnetic powers, to build a temple dedicated to Arsinöe, the wife of Ptolemy Philadelphus, the roof of which was to be made of lodestone so that the iron statue of the Queen might remain suspended as if floating in the air. The artist unfortunately did not live to complete his design.

Ancient Buddhists were convinced that the sapphire would open barred doors and dwellings (for the spirit of Man). It produces a desire for prayer and brings with it more peace than any other gem, but he who would wear it must lead a pure and holy life.

An interesting legend is that of the Lee Penny. This famous penny is a precious jewel, but to what class it belongs is not known. The reason for it being called the Lee Penny is because its owners were the Lockhart family of Lee Castle in the Vale of Clyde and the jewel was set in the centre of an old English silver coin. It was supposed to be efficacious in diseases of horned cattle, the procedure being to dangle the Penny on a chain, dip it into water three times, give it a swirl and the cattle drinking the water had a speedy cure.

In the reign of Charles 1, the people of Newcastle being afflicted with the plague, sent for and obtained the loan of the Lee Penny, leaving the sum of £ 6,000 sterling in its place as a pledge. They found it so effectual, or were so impressed with its powers, that they proposed to keep it and forfeit the money. But the Laird of Lee would not consent to part with so gifted a family heirloom.

A few years after the stone was returned from Newcastle, a complaint was lodged against Sir James Lockhart on account of "the superstitious using of a stone set in silver for curing of diseased cattle". This came before the Synod of Glasgow and resulted in the fact that they recognised its peculiar virtues and the Laird was permitted to continue using it. It could be that Sir Walter Scott founded his novel "The Talisman" upon the above fact, as it antedates his work by many centuries.

The idea that the brilliancy of gems varies in sympathy with the health of the wearer is very well known and seems to belong to all of the precious stones, but is more pronounced in the more valuable. In the case of the ruby it is stated that it gives a warning by a change of colour when misfortune is about to befall its wearer.

Wolfgangus Gabelschwerus said he had personal experience of the ruby changing its colour. "On the Fifth of December, 1600, as I was going with my beloved wife Catherina from Stuttgard to Cabina, I noticed that a very fine ruby, which I wore in a ring given to me by Catherina, lost repeatedly its colour, assuming a sombre blackish hue. This lasted over several days. I drew the ring from my finger and placed it in a casket. I warned my wife that some evil followed her or me and truly I was not deceived, for within a few days she was taken mortally sick. After her death the ruby resumed its normal colour and brilliance.

John Aubery in his "Miscellanies" mentions an occult principle inherent in the beryl stone, that of inducing clairvoyance. He quotes several reliable authorities for his statement. One such was Sir Marmaduke Langdale, he looked into one when in Italy and foretold events that came true.

A delightful myth is told about the origin of amber. "The daughters of Apollo were so grief-stricken at the death of their brother Phaeton that the Gods changed them into poplars, so that their sorrow might be forgotten. It came about that they remembered, and beautiful tears of amber exuded from the barks.

The ammonite or snake stone is not

so well known, but nevertheless it has a legend attached to it. A variety of this stone called the Horn of Ammon placed under the pillow at night gives prophetic or divine dreams.

In ancient Mexico the opal was the most sacred of stones and said to contain the soul of truth. It is the stone of the hermits and the gem of the Gods who live alone. The Mexicans claimed that it was the soul of fire which created worlds and men.

The Japanese used to, and may even to this day, commune with their Deity by gazing intently on a large globe of pure crystal placed in the centre of the room, the family sitting around on mats with a fixed gaze upon the stone. The answer to their petitions and desires comes through the crystal.

The ruby is the sacred stone of the Burmese who liken it to a human soul about to enter the sacred precincts of Buddha, and consequently, in the last stage of transmigration before entering the eternal embrace of Divine Love.

In olden days magicians wore a ring which they called the "ring of strength" containing seven gems, a ruby, emerald, selenite, amethyst, onyx, turquoise and agate. As a centrestone the magician concerned used his birth stone, the other stones set in a circle around it. Wear it and fear no man, "for thou wilt be invincible as Achilles", says Philadelphus.

There have been many legends woven round the diamond, perhaps more than round any other gem, but one of the most facinating can be found in ancient Babylonian teachings. "A diamond was hanging around Abraham's neck and a sick man looking upon it was cured. When Abraham passed away the Lord sealed it in the planet of the Sun".

The diamond's reputed power of binding man and woman together in happy marriage has made it a popular stone for engagement rings, however looking at the divorce figures this too would appear to be a lovely legend!

In India many of the Yogis wear a ruby on the forehead where the third eye is supposed to be. According to the Yogis this aids them in sending mental impressions over long distances. There may be a certain amount of truth in this legend as it has now been discovered that the ruby can be used in radio equipment and it assists in the transmission of broadcasts over very long distances.

The topaz is reputed to have the vibrations that will open the door to communications and impressions sent by those who have crossed over into the after life.

Native pearl divers who gather in the oysters that produce this stone believe that it has the power to ward off evil and protect them from sharks if worn while diving.

All down the ages the amethyst has been associated with wine, presumably because of its colour. It is only to be expected with this association that there would be a myth involving Bacchus with the amethyst.

In some manner Bacchus had been offended and in an act of revenge he decided to set tigers on the first person who should cross his path. The first person to do so was a pure and gentle maiden by the name of Amethyst, she was on her way to worship at the shrine of Diana. As the tigers sprang towards her she cried to the Goddess to save her. In order to save Amethyst, Diana turned the terrified girl into pure white stone. Bacchus repented at what he had done and to show his regret he poured juice of the grape over her. Amethyst's lifeless figure took on the rather lovely colour we know today as amethyst.

Cleopatra was supposed to have an amethyst ring that had engraved upon it a likeness of the God Mithras.

The aquamarine in the Middle Ages was used for fortune telling, suspended by thread over a bowl of water. Around the edge of the bowl were the letters of the alphabet and when asked a question the aquamarine would spell out the answer to it by swinging of its own accord to letter after letter in a similar manner to the ouija board activity.

The sacred Kalpa tree of the Hindus, which is used as a symbolic offering to the Gods, has been reputed to consist of gemstones. Pearls hang from its boughs, emeralds from its shoots, the young leaves are formed of coral and the ripe fruit from rubies, the roots are of sapphire and the lower trunk of diamonds, the upper trunk is of cats-eye and the foliage is composed of zircon.

Emeralds, according to one ancient legend, were said to have originated in the "Nests of Griffons". It has been carried down the ages in legend that God gave four emeralds to Solomon that he might have wisdom and rule the four quarters of creation.

A legend from the Talmud states that Noah's ark was illuminated by one perfectly cut garnet and that it acted as a guiding light as soon as darkness fell.

An ancient Jewish legend records that a city built by Abraham, as an expression of devotion to Hagar, had such high walls around it that the light could not penetrate. Abraham gave his six sons large precious stones of every description. According to the legend they were so bright that no other source of light was needed.

The Hindus at one time, and maybe still do so to this day, used the ammonite in their religious ceremonies and believed that if placed next to the death bed of a person dying it would introduce his soul to the deities.

South Sea Islanders used the beryl as a rainmaker and maintained that it was equally efficacious in bringing drought on their enemies.

It is a legendary belief that the Stone-of-Memphis applied to any part of the body which is essential to operate preserves that part from any pain in the operation.

The rock crystal is held in high regard in some branches of Buddhism. According to the Tibetan system one region of heaven (the eastern) is built of white crystal. The western region is of ruby.

Bramah repenting of a sin he had commited was in such grief that a hot tear fell from him to the earth and so was the first sapphire formed.

Part of the myth and legend attached to the gemstones are the astrological correspondences which include planetary as well as Zodiacal attributes.

The planetary correspondences are as follows:-

Sun
Sunstone, Ruby, Diamond, Topaz.

Moon
Moonstone, Selenite, Pearl, Labradonite.

Mercury
Chrysolite, Rock Crystal, Aquamarine

Mars
Lodestone, Mexican Fire Opal, Garnet

Venus
Lapis Lazuli, Sapphire, Turquoise.

Jupiter
Carbuncle, Emerald, Beryl.

Saturn
Onyx, Jet, Carnelian, Chalcedony.

Earth
Agate, Bloodstone, Moss Agate.

Uranus
Opal, Tourmaline.

Neptune
Amethyst, Coral.

Stones vary in their temperament according to the astrological or group of astrological signs to which they are related. From the group aspect stones related under element groups have a nature befitting the signs in that group. These are as follows:-

Stones under the Fire Group, Aries, Leo and Sagittarius:-   Hot and dry.

Stones under the Earth Group, Taurus, Virgo and Capricorn:-   Cold and dry.

Stones under the Air Group, Gemini, Libra and Aquarius:-   Hot and humid.

Stones under the Water Group, Cancer, Scorpio and Pisces:-   Cold and humid.

Many different correspondences of gems to the astrological signs have been given over the years, until great confusion and divergence of opinion has arisen.

To arrive at the correct birthday stone for each sign there are two considerations, the gemstones of the High Priest's breastplate, the original twelve, and if taken in order they produce the following relationships:-

Aries:	Bloodstone
Taurus:	Lapis lazuli
Gemini:	Agate
Cancer:	Emerald
Leo:	Onyx
Virgo:	Cornelian
Libra:	Chrysolite
Scorpio:	Beryl
Sagittarius:	Topaz
Capricorn:	Turquoise
Aquarius:	Garnet
Pisces:	Amethyst

115

The second consideration is the correspondence of gemstones to the months of the year, which are as follows:

Month	Gemstone
January:	Garnet
February:	Amethyst
March:	Bloodstone
April:	Lapis Lazuli
May:	Agate
June:	Emerald
July:	Ruby
August:	Onyx
September:	Chrysolite
October:	Beryl
November:	Topaz
December:	Turquoise

A close examination of these two tables will show that some individuals have a birthstone that corresponds to their sign and the month in which they were born, but others have two birthstones, that appropriate to their sign and the one for the month, due to the sign of the Zodiac covering two months.

An individual born in March under the sign of Aries would only have the bloodstone as his birthstone, but if he was born in April under the sign of Aries, he would have the choice of two stones, that of the sign, the bloodstone, and the one for the month, Lapis Lazuli.

It might be well to mention here that some gems have over the centuries changed their names. The sapphire as a birthstone is non-existant if we refer to the sapphire of today. The sapphire of the ancients and of biblical times was the stone we know today as the lapis lazuli.

It is shown in the tables of correspondences so that there will be no misunderstanding. The agate and onyx were also known by different names, but the stones as listed are those of the breastplate, the old names.

So that those who are interested in their birthstone can find it at a glance, the following table has been compiled overleaf:-

	Aries	Taurus	Gemini
	Bloodstone	Lapis Lazuli	Agate
Mar:	Bloodstone		
Apr:	Lapis Lazuli	Lapis Lazuli	
May:		Agate	Agate
Jun:			Emerald
Jul:			
Aug:			
Sep:			
Oct:			
Nov:			
Dec:			
Jan:			
Feb:			

	Cancer	Leo	Virgo
	Emerald	Onyx	Carnelian
Mar:			
Apr:			
May:			
Jun:	Emerald		
Jul:	Ruby	Ruby	
Aug:		Onyx	Onyx
Sep;			Chrysolite
Oct:			
Nov:			
Dec:			
Jan:			
Feb:			

	Libra	Scorpio	Sagittarius
	Chrysolite	Beryl	Topaz
Mar:			
Apr:			
May:			
Jun:			
Jul:			
Aug:			
Sep:	Chrysolite		
Oct:	Beryl	Beryl	
Nov:		Topaz	Topaz
Dec:			Turquoise
Jan:			
Feb:			

	Capricorn	Aquarius	Pisces
	Turquoise	Garnet	Amethyst
Mar:			
Apr:			
May:			
Jun:			
Jul:			
Aug:			
Sep:			
Oct:			
Nov:			
Dec:	Turquoise		
Jan:	Garnet	Garnet	
Feb:		Amethyst	Amethyst

121

Where there are two stones available the first choice should always be the stone of the Zodiacal sign.

One of the reasons for confusion over birthstones is due to occult teachings giving correspondences of gem stones to the Rays. Each sign of the Zodiac emits its own particular Ray and these Rays have an affinity with the gem stones.

It is possible to have a very long list of gem stones that are attached to a specific Ray, but the gem stones of the Rays are not birthstones.

A further confusing factor is that occultisis have worked on the basis of seven Rays and not the twelve, and so there are stones allocated to a sign that have no affinity with that sign at all.

So that a complete picture is shown, the next table gives twelve Rays and their corresponding gems.

Silver Ray

At the highest level silver and at the lowest dark grey with all the various shades in between. The gem stones of this Ray are: zircon, ostiocolla, ostracites, marcasite, falcones, filaterius, pumex or punicus, pyrites, moonstone, sarcophagus, talk alchimicus, grey pearl and blue-lace agate.

White Ray

Alectoria, amianthus, beloculus, chrysolyte, white coral, crystal, cysteolithos, enydros or eryndros, fingites, galatides, iris, kabrates, kaman or kakaman, lignites, limacie, pearl, quartz, ranius or rabri, rock crystal, samius, unicorn or ceratites, zarites.

Black Ray

Andromantes, black coral, dionysia, gargates, haematite, jet, lode stone, medus, nephrite, onyx, radaim, samothracia, black pearl.

Amethyst Ray

Amethyst, balasius, ethices, or endes, exebonos, falcones, kinocetus, blue john.

Purple Ray

Balasius, blue john, demonius, heliotrope, hyacinth, jacinth.

Red Ray

Anthracites, balasius, bezoar or beza, bloodstone, carbuncle, red coral,

emathitis, epistides, fongates, garatronicus, garnet, red jasper, onicinus,
fire opal, pink pearl, ruby, sardius.

Brown Ray

Agate, alectoria, bronia, bufonite,
carnelian, blue john, brown coral,
jasper, raninsor, rabri, sardonyx,
tigers eye.

Indigo Ray

Exebonos, filaterius, lapis lazuli,
selenites or sirites, specular stone.

Orange Ray

Amber, cats eye, crisonterinus,
hamonis, tigers eye, topaz.

Green Ray

Emerald, malachite, jade, moss
agate, peridot, chrysoprase, chrysoberyl, alexandrite, tourmaline, beryl,
chalcedony.

Blue Ray

Sapphire, turquoise, aquamarine,

blue diamond, blue topaz, beryl, blue pearl.

Yellow Ray

Chrysoberyl, citrine, yellow pearl, chalcedony.

There are, of course, many other stones, but the preceeding table is a guide.

Apart from finding the correct birthstone some people may like to work with the stone for the day:-

Sunday:	Sunstone
Monday:	Moonstone
Tuesday:	Ruby
Wednesday:	Citrine
Thursday:	Amethyst
Friday:	Sapphire
Saturday:	Onyx

To obtain the maximum benefit from each stone choose the right day of the right month in which to wear it. As an example of this ancient gem lore, to make the most of the amethyst qualities it should be worn on a Thursday in February when Pisces is ruling.

Certain gemstones are connected to the senses and can therefore be of use in developing or making the senses more sensitive. Chrysoprase will help the sense of balance, jacinth-speech, the topaz for the sense of taste and jasper for smell. Sardonyx will sharpen the hearing and the chalcedony increases the sensitivity of touch.

There are seven planetary principles to seven stones, and of course there are seven planetary principles to the seven lower sephiroth on the Kabbalistic Tree of Life. The stones relating to these principles are sapphire, ruby, chrysolite, emerald, amethyst, moonstone and onyx.

It is known that the ancient Kabbalists took gemstones into consideration in their studies and rituals. The old Kabbalists looked upon the chrysoprase as a solar stone. They also used chrysolite with gold in performing solar operations and the moonstone with silver for lunar operations.

Further aspects of talismanic magic of Kabbalism refers the agate to the influence of Mercury, wherein is the gift of counsel and power over eloquence, poetry, music, astronomy and mathematics. The amethyst is referred to divination and relates it to the planet

Mars with the gift of force, though its influence is operative in peace, friendship, sincerity and grandeur of the soul.

The chalcedony is related to and connected with the transcendental sciences and the contemplation of divine things, whilst the carbuncle was looked upon as being in kinship with all magnificence and royal majesty.

Apart from all other divisions that have been made there is still the further divisions of "Stones and the Elements" and "Stones and the Seasons".

Stones belonging to the element of Air are diamond, opal, chrysolite, kaman, lacteus, mirites, turchion and the urim and thumim.

Those related to the element of Fire are ruby, bloodstone, topaz, tigers eye, sunstone, bezoar, jasper, spinel and solis gemma.

Related to Water are the following: aquamarine, selenites, sapphire, pearl, coral and, of course, the moonstone.

There are many related to the element of Earth, the following are just a few of them: agate, carnelian, sardonyx, onyx, zircon, nephrite, blue john and malachite.

The divisions of the seasons are quite simple. Spring: all green and blue stones. Summer: all the gold and yellow. Autumn: all the reddish brown and red stones. Winter: all black and brown.

If it were desired to wear a different stone each day, the gems given to each day can be converted into a talisman irrespective of the birth data. They would be as follows:

Sunday

A ruby or chrysolite set in gold and engraved either on the stone or the gold a sceptred king upon a lion, or a queen with a sceptre, for a woman.

Monday

A selenite, pearl or opal set in silver. The design engraved on either stone or silver should be a king riding on a doe, or a woman with a bow and arrow, for a woman.

Tuesday

An amethyst or bloodstone, set in iron. The design would be a king on a wolf or a female warrior.

Wednesday

An olivine, agate or jade set in platinum, with a design of a king riding upon a bear, or a woman spinning.

Thursday

An emerald or sapphire set in tin, with a design of a king with a javelin riding on a stag, or a woman bedecked with flowers

Friday

A turquoise, beryl or lapis lazuli set in copper. The design should be a king on a camel or a naked maiden.

Saturday

An onyx set in lead. The design for this amulet is a king crowned and seated on a dragon. For a woman it should be a witch.

Apart from the amulets mentioned above there are also talismanic gems which, according to ancient teachings, had affinity with a specific Archangel or Guardian Angel. These are as follows:

Gabriel; onyx.   Barchiel: Jasper

Malchediel: ruby.   Ashmodel: Topaz

Amriel: carbuncle. Muriel: Emerald

Verchiel: sapphire. Hamatiel: Sardonyx

Isumiel: jacinth.   Bariel: Agate

Adnachiel: amethyst. Humiel: Beryl

Gemstones are also related to specific wedding anniversaries, but not until the twelfth anniversary is reached

129

and then the stones are related as
follows:

Anniversary	12	-	agate
"	13	-	moonstone
"	14	-	moss agate
"	15	-	rock crystal
"	16	-	topaz
"	17	-	amethyst
"	18	-	garnet
"	19	-	zircon
"	23	-	sapphire
"	30	-	pearl
"	35	-	coral
"	40	-	ruby
"	55	-	emerald

To the Chinese, jade symbolises
the five cardinal virtues, courage,
modesty, charity, wisdom and justice,
and so is both the betrothal and anniversary stone of all wedding anniversaries.

NOTES